iPhone 11 I

A Handy Guide to Learn about Detailed Functions and Features of Your iPhone

By

Albrecht Meyer

The information provided herein is stated to be truthful and consistent, in that any liability, in terms of inattention or otherwise, by any usage or abuse of any policies, processes, or directions contained within is the solitary and utter responsibility of the recipient reader. Under no circumstances will any legal responsibility or blame be held against the publisher for any reparation, damages, or monetary loss due to the information herein, either directly or indirectly.

Respective authors own all copyrights not held by the publisher.

The information herein is offered for informational purposes solely, and is universal as so. The presentation of the information is without contract or any type of guarantee assurance.

The trademarks that are used are without any consent, and the publication of the trademark is without permission or backing by the trademark owner. All trademarks and brands within this book are for clarifying purposes only and are owned by the owners themselves, not affiliated with this document.

Table of contents

INTRODUCTION.. 7

CHAPTER 1: HISTORY AND EVOLUTION
OF IPHONE... 13

1.1 History of the iPhone and its Evolution..................... 14

1.2 Evolution from iPhone 11 to 11 Pro........................... 23

1.3 Modern Technology and Usage of iPhone 29

CHAPTER 2: IPHONE 11 PRO-
SPECIFICATIONS, FEATURES, AND
FUNCTIONS... 35

2.1 Design 37

2.2 Display... 40

2.3 A13 Bionic Processor 41

2.4 True Depth Camera and Face Id 43

2.5 Triple-Lens Rear Camera 47

2.6 Battery Life... 53

2.7 Connectivity... 54

2.8 Phone Set up, Apps, and Other Features 58

CHAPTER 3: CONSUMER REVIEWS AND
AVAILABILITY....................................... 68

3.1 Consumer Verdict by Apple and the Benefits Associated 69

3.2 User Reviews 71

3.3 Pricing and Warranty 74

3.4 Availability and Other Related Products 74

CHAPTER 4: CHALLENGES FACED BY EMERGING IOS 13 TECHNOLOGY 77

4.1 Get ready for 13.5.5 and 13.5.1 79

4.2 New in iOS 13.4 and 13.4.1 81

4.3 New iOS 13.3.1 issues 83

4.4 New in iOS 13.3 84

4.5 iOS 13.2 and iOS 13.1.3 87

4.6 iOS 13 issues originally 92

CHAPTER 5: ADDITIONAL TIPS AND TRICKS TO USE IPHONE 11 PRO 100

5.1 Safari and iCloud Tips 101

5.2 Home Screen and Display 102

5.3 Messages, Emoji and Keyboard Tips 106

5.4 Camera and Photos 114

5.5 Control Centre and Lock Screen Tips 117

5.6 Notifications and Restrictions.......................................**121**

5.7 Battery and Wireless Charging Explained................**123**

5.8 Notes, Maps, and Apple Music Tips..........................**123**

5.9 Buttons, Gesture, and Control....................................**129**

5.10 Payment Tips for Apple **130**

CONCLUSION...**131**

Introduction

Have you ever said, "When was the very first iPhone Apple launched," or wondered, "How did the first mobile originate?" There is the whole past of iPhone creation in this essay. Two thousand and twenty prints to mark the thirteenth celebration of the world's first iPhone update, so the worldwide development of iPhone models starting 2007 is commended for iPhone and Apple products. Since Apple provided an iPhone, the one that came was more than 3 G mobile connectivity, and the iPhone 2 was missing. Okay, Apple hopped straight on top of it to iPhone X. In the last few years, apple manufacturing has pushed up to now twenty iPhones, including the iPhones 3, 4, 5, iPhone S and iPhone Plus, including the new iPhone 11 and iPhone SE extension (smartphones from the second era).

In the ongoing month of September, Apple gave a few iOS updates for iPhone XS, XS Max, and XR individually, including 11, 11 Pro and 11 Pro Max. Those mobile-phones which are new comprising of significantly improved screens, have an amazing processor blasting, and, in general, increasingly strong development quality.

For review iPhone 11, starting at $699 demonstrated $50 less expensive than the iPhone XR, which was its underlying cost when it was propelled.

Among the iPhone range, it is quite elusive which one the customer will pick either is 11, 11 Pro, or 11 Pro Max. Every one of these smartphones involves similar handling frameworks, similar highlights, such as focal and ultra-wide front cameras running iOS 13. Though really, (iPhone 11) Pro and Pro Max seem to be comparable in pretty much every viewpoint, aside from quality, weight, battery working hours, and other features. The iPhone 11 is perhaps the most significant expense for an exceptional telephone that you will buy now, and it has a great part of a similar 11 Pro applications. Contrary to this iPhone 11 Pro comprises of various essential changes to make it the largest iPhone ever constructed. For $999, it is likewise beginning at $300 more than the iPhone 11.

The new iPhone models from Apple include an impressive 6.5 inch (OLED) Multi-Touch Screen Super Retina XDR or 5.8 inches (iPhone 11 Pro). It acts as the viewfinder for the Camera app, which helps you to view your pictures beautifully in the Photos feature.

Based on the version of iPhones 11 Pro or 11 Pro Max, you have 256 GB, 64 GB, or 512 GB of total internal storage. You can now connect a flash drive to your smartphone's Lightning port and then upload or archive your digital picture with this external storage feature. You will potentially optimize internal storage space inside your iPhone by choosing to use the iCloud Picture Library in accordance with your iCloud (online-based) profile. You will read more about selecting the Camera and Photos applications menu choices later in this article. Optimize iPhone Space is a tool that can be used to optimize internal image capacity on your device.

The iPhone 11 Pro targets those who want everything Apple can do on a device. It is the best of those available by apple products, with prices reflecting that. They have had pretty much the same apps in the particular price range and screen size.

All iPhone 11 Pro models give you the brightest and most colorful screen that Apple has to offer. In addition to ultra-wide and wide-angle lenses, the phones have an additional 2x optical zoom image sensor.

This is a great option, with steel fronts rather than plastic than many Apple items that give it a luxurious grip.

Yet it has a lifetime battery life and is stronger water resistance relative to iPhone XR and iPhone SE, and you will have no fear about your handset slipping into the tub or leaking water by accident.

iPhone 11 Pro Max and 11 Pro are the newest, state of the art iPhone from Apple. The Apple iPhone 11pro's most common applications include digital images, recording, and storage, printing, and sharing. Optical and digital zoom features built into iPhone cameras and the camera app enable up to 10x images to be zoomed. The front and rear cameras will now utilize iOS 13 portrait shooting as well as Portrait Lighting functionality (which now has six separate effects as you will soon find out). The iOS 13 version contains a brand new Night Mode, enhanced red-eye adjustment, better video live apps, object geography, auto picture stabilization, a revised Burst shooting. The iPhone 11Pro smartphones deliver 1, 12MP (megapixel), True depth camera on the front, and three back, 12-megapixel cameras – one with an ultra-wide-angle lens, a telephoto lens, and one wide-angle lens.

The device from the iPhone series has a 5.8-inch display that convinces many who consider the iPhone SE to be small and that the iPhone 11 Pro, iPhone XR are too large relative to this. This ends at 999 bucks.

The iPhone 11 is a phenomenal arrangement at the unit's cost, second just to the iPhone SE 2020. Following the 2018 iPhone XR strides, Apple astutely presented the 11 as an iPhone for most clients. Given the decreased nature of the Oled board, the iPhone 11 series have equivalent A13 CPU with a nearly similar setup for the camera as the version of the improved 11 Plus series. This additionally comes in six unmistakable shades, opposed the CNET lessening and water resistance checks, and got the CNET Editors' Choice Award.

iPhone 11 Pro is most popular in the series of iPhone giving purchasers updates, including high-goal OLED show, a finishing of matte-glass, and a tempered steel sideband, VIP treatment is given. This has another back camera that works with Apple's ongoing deep fusion features in picture handling, which is taking superb zoomed-in pictures. The most basic change to 11 Pro is that it possesses long battery life as compared to the past model iPhone XS.

Maybe the clearest and huge avocation for buying the iPhone 11 pro over the iPhone 11 is the cost. They are distinctive size items, so they sit diversely in your pockets.

The iPhone 11 Pro series, as compared to others, is small among all iPhone 11 cell phones with a 5.8-inch screen and at least 6.63 ounces.

The strong inclination handset is the most simple one-gave device to utilize. With a weight of 6.84 ounces, iPhone 11 is thicker than 11 Plus, yet it is not heavily weighted. iPhone 11 is 0.2 millimeters more plentiful as compared to 11 Pro, which causes it to feel somewhat stout.

The hands and wishes of each are a person. Be that as it may, in case you are ready to forfeit a heavyweight on a greater edge, get the 11 and spare $300. Also, in the event that you need without a doubt the gigantic screen, you can get a $1,099 iPhone 11 Max with an OLED board of 6.5-inch, having a weight of 7.97 ounces.

Chapter 1: History and Evolution of iPhone

Have you, at any point, let yourself know, "Which was the very first iPhone introduced by Apple to come out" or considered the question that "How the first smartphone came into existence?" There is the whole history of iPhone formation, which is discussed in this chapter. Two thousand twenty imprints to be the thirteenth commemoration of the first iPhone discharge around the world, so the advancement of iPhone models beginning in 2007 is commended worldwide for the achievement of iPhone and items by apple.

Do you know there is no iPhone 2 here? Since Apple delivered an iPhone in the main form, the one that followed since it was more for 3 G portable access, and the iPhone 2 was missed. Shouldn't something be said about the iPhone 9? All right, Apple jumped on top of it and straight into iPhone X. Throughout these recent years, the technology of apple has propelled 20 iPhones up until now, including iPhone 3, 4, 5, iPhone S, and iPhone Plus variants, among them with the new expansion of iPhone 11 range and iPhone SE (second era smartphones).

In this chapter, there is an exhaustive discussion on the historical backdrop of the iOS, starting with Steve Jobs presenting the first iPhone. This chapter explores the evolutionary history of iOS in detail, beginning with Steve Jobs' first iPhone presentation.

As time progresses, iPhone owners and sweets have found the benefit of ensuring the device situation by demonstrating the complexity of each program, which makes it easy to discover the global world through clicking. Could you think that 16 Tb is what you can load on your iPhone? The iPhone 3 G is certainly not changed from the original iPhone.

1.1 History of the iPhone and its Evolution

As time advances, it has gone to considering iPhone proprietors and darlings that they have the advantage of improving the computerized condition by presenting the scope of individual applications that make it simple to explore the global world through tapping.

Nonetheless, the emphasis was on an app store, which was introduced afterward! The new iPhone launch had 3 G, which proved that you could use the internet without taking action to chuck the phone around the room. Apple's first iPhone launched ten years ago, — 29 June 2007 — for the next week.

While not the first product, it jumped over the market and ignited a creative revolution.This chapter's observations demonstrate part of the big implications of the flexible blast over previous centuries of the iPhone-driven — and Google-driven App. Steve Jobs downloaded the iPhone only because he described it as "a wireless breakthrough," "a large screen iPod with the highlights of touch control," and an "advanced web-information tool."

- iPhone:

Would you be able to envision that 16 GB is what you should stack on your underlying iPhone? Without a doubt, there is not much information that can be saved on the iPhone yet, and positively not the App Store settings were in this. Nonetheless, you had connections to the web on a PC so you could see it. In addition to this, you could oblige just 128 MB of smash files. The sensor is worth 2.0 megapixels — along these lines, wrong. However, you have a PC with a camera! God, Holy Moly!

- 3 G iPhone:

Undoubtedly, the iPhone 3 G has not transformed from the underlying iPhone. However, the focus was the new addition was an App Store, which was subsequently added in this addition! The new edition of the iPhone got 3 G, which demonstrated that you could utilize the web without taking steps to hurl the iPhone around the house.

- 3GS iPhone:

Apple has propelled an iPhone 3GS 32 GB stockpiling elective. The approach of the Application Store has improved features in this phone. Between pictures, tunes, and mobile phones, 16 GB simply wasn't enough for the users to use. In this phone, the sensor was refreshed to 3 MP and consolidated video feature. Apple Company has introduced Voice Recognition feature also, yet we'd need to hang tight a couple more years for Siri to be propelled.

- iPhone 4:

At last, we are attempting to go there. The iPhone 4 is viewed as among the first cell phone to highlight a forward-looking camera on it. Little was done by Apple imagine that the selfies will assume control over the planet. The iPhone 4 likewise incorporates an eye camera. At 512 MB storage, it was intended to be a better phone than the iPhone 3GS, which had 256 MB storage. With the addition of these features, the iPhone camera was giving a more natural touch, yet 32 GB became the most elevated measure of limit that the iPhone could oblige.

- iPhone 4S:

Discussion relating to the gigantic contrast among iPhone 4 and iPhone 4S: camera specs started from 5 MP up to 8 MP. Today, this is an update. Apple has now propelled the 64 GB stockpiling model yet has held the slam at 512 MB. At that point in this addition, the video could be recorded in 1080 pixels. Goodness, in this, we cannot overlook. During its first week, Apple dispatched 4,000,000 iPhone 4S gadgets.

- iPhone 5:

Apple transported 5 million iPhone 5 gadgets in the first week of launch. The picture remained equivalent, yet the limit was improved up to 1 GB. Do not you think 3 G feature was cool? Above, this company decided to push the iPhone 5 with the addition of an LTE network. Apple has likewise presented an iPhone 5 Lightning connector. The screens in the past models had 3.5 inches. However, the iPhone 5 had a screen of 4 inches.

- iPhone 5s and iPhone 5c:

Apple delivered 9,000,000 gadgets in the main seven day stretch of dispatch between iPhone 5s and iPhone 5c. iPhone 5c was proposed to be the better version in terms of its efficiency with its plastic body. This iPhone had four distinct shades. However, not more features were introduced. Then again, iPhone 5s included some new features such as Touch ID, a concurrent camera with moderate movement recording. In addition to these features, it also included the M7 movement co-processor, which opened up a wide universe of conceivable outcomes helping the moderate life of the battery.

- iPhone 6 and 6 Plus:

Steve jobs and apple seems to roll out more improvements from the current emphasis and the S form than it does from the S variant to the most recent update. The inner iPhone 6 applications are supposed to be similar to those of iPhone 5s. The distinction in this version was a lot bigger screen, which as compared to the previous one, which is now called 6 Plus. The Eye show camera has become HD, and an iPhone with 128 GB of capacity has been introduced. However, the slam volume continued as before, so the gadget did not have megapixel support.

- iPhone 6s and 6s Plus:

All right, nothing was added. Everything was similar stuff. Yet, inside, Apple has updated iPhone 6s within a considerable amount. The framework took a gigantic hop forward from 8

Mega Pixels to 12 Mega Pixels. The storage has likewise been expanded from 1 GB to 2 GB. Since iPhone 6 made them with twisted issues, Apple sent the iPhone 6s 7000 Aluminum Series to ensure it does not happen ever again. To wrap things up, the 3D Interaction has also been included.

- iPhone SE:

Try not to assume that you have pondered the SE iPhone. It contains all the astounding inward highlights of iPhone 6s out of a little box without a 3D screen. In any case, by and large, the iPhone SE has been presented as an increasingly moderate choice that individuals adored.

- iPhone 7 and 7 Plus:

In the long run, Apple has planned an alternative 16 GB base edition, with iPhone 7 and iPhone 7 Plus basic versions starting from the range of 32 GB to 256 GB. Another polished Jet Black paint has been powered by Apple. iPhone 7 Plus is more traditional than previous plus modifications thanks to the new breakthrough in double-camera, allowing a dramatically better zoom in and out capability possible. Imaging mode feature is a product overhaul that allows iPhone 7 Plus customers to take pleasant images with Depth of Field. Perhaps Apple's expelled earphone port was the most destructive component of the iPhone 7 and 7 Plus. Ear Pods attached to the lightning port and standard earphone adapter have been followed by new iPhones. Apple simultaneously showed the remote Air Pods when it sensed the cancelation of the earphone port.

- iPhone 8 and 8 Plus:

iPhone 8 and 8 Plus joined remote accusing of a glass shield on the phone's backside. The camera was incredible, with programming for altering and screening photographs. The whole tone screen expanded the client experience by powerfully raising the affectability to blue light. Individuals steadily became used to not utilizing an earphone attachment and started changing to their convenient ways.

- iPhone X:

Discussing cool pictures, iPhone X includes an extra forward-looking camera that helps take wonderful selfies in Portrait mode. Truly, some iPhones allow taking some incredible looking pictures. However, iPhone X highlighted Portrait mode alternative accessible for the forward-looking camera with experienced, passionate feelings from the start.

- iPhone XS and XS Max:

Avoiding directly past iPhone 9, Apple discharged XS and XS Max by the Steve Jobs Theater in September 2018. Such forms were very much named because they were free updates in the series of iPhone X. The two adaptations had a forward-looking picture mode selfie telephone. The screens were side to the base, so they looked astounding with the Super Eye HD camera. The biggest change in this new edition might be the littlest; the A12 bionic processor supported the figuring limit while developing the battery channel.

- iPhone XR:

iPhone XR was introduced in September 2018 assembling however was not accessible right away. Since the most recent adaptations were less expensive, many individuals needed to trust that the XR will be qualified. These iPhone models were littler when contrasted with the XS and the XS Peak. The screen does not seem as brilliant as the XS and XS Max, yet the hole was not very noteworthy with the Liquid Retina HD board. That release even had a forward-looking webcam that came in a larger number of hues than XS or XS Max.

- iPhone 11:

Within Apple's yearly plan, iPhone 11 is the least costly. This still has ample modern functionality to deal with the strongest iPhone in 2019. The Machine features a 6.1 "Liquid Retina," which monitors and accepts both hues. The second rear camera is an impressive 12 mm upgrade, with massive, ultra-wide focus points.

- iPhone 11 Pro:

For clients searching for a little telephone with a first in the class show in the Apple item extend, iPhone 11 Pro is for them. 5.8-inch Super Eye (retina) XDR screen is the most splendid and straightforward Apple PC to date. This phone sport has just two, however, three, 12 MP HDR camera focal points with standard, ultra-wide, and zooming focal points. Shading decisions are quieter than the iPhone 11.

- iPhone 11 X Plus:

iPhone 11 Pro Max is Apple's latest and costly 2019 smartphone. As in 11 Pro, the panel is Apple's Super Eye (Retina) XDR. The screen is, however, 6.5-inch. The Pro Max has the same 3-point camera setup as the 11 Pro, with a related shading judgment, rendering the scale almost as the single difference between the gadgets.

- iPhone SE (second era):

Apple is incorporating several experiments from the past for this tradition of the iPhone. 4.7-inch eye (Retina) HD panel and Home Touch ID capture will return to the underlying SE at a similarly low fee. The second SE variant includes the full spectrum of Apple's most costly iPhones, including the new Portrait and Depth Control software technology with A13 Bionic Cpu, a chronicle of the finest standard, lengthy battery life and remote storage.

- Generations of iOS to Come:

As you are able to see, the iPhone had many updates, varying from a 16 GB Web interface to a 512 GB monitor, work area, and entertainment content. We wanted to hear about the iPhone's history, so we believe you did it! Make sure you get back in and keep up with all new ways as the iPhone continues to evolve and expand.

1.2 Evolution from iPhone 11 to 11 Pro

The iPhone 11 Pro and 11 share much of the same structures, but still, there are several main model variations, as the iPhone 11 is much cheaper. Below, we have mentioned the two smartphones with all their apps, and you can see on a glance what is new and the same.

iPhone 11 Pro vs. iPhone 11: Display

iPhone 11 utilizes LCD technology, and the two Pro versions utilize advanced OLED technology. The inexpensive iPhone 11 has a bigger screen than the iPhone 11 Pro, but its output is smaller.

We have not checked the phones yet, and it is not easy to explain how such screens feel. Yet clearly depending on the image size and what we learn about Apple's OLEDs, the Pro versions should show darker black and lighter colors. The Advanced versions also improve the iPhone11 Advanced with the A13 Bionic Cpu.

- iPhone 11 Pro: 5.8-inch Super Retina XDR, 2436 x 1125
- iPhone 11: 6.1-inch Liquid Retina, 1792 x 828
- iPhone 11 Pro Max: 6.5-inch Super Retina XDR, 2688 x 1242

iPhone 11 Pro vs. iPhone 11: Front camera

Both versions of the iPhone 11 pro and iPhone 11 have a 12MP and f/2.2 opening sensor. The three versions all display the Apple True Depth Camera, including Face ID. Apple introduced a completely new display: "Slofie."

iPhone 11 Pro vs. iPhone 11: Design

The sandwiched iPhone 11 is between the iPhone 11 Standard and the Standard Avg. The three feature a fresh square camera setup on the same coated monitor and glass back. The 11 Pros have sides made of steel, and the cheaper iPhone 11 has edges made of aluminum.

iPhone 11 also consists of the same square image boost as the Max, but it has only two lenses. The Pro Max has a smaller panel and a reinforced frame. These three iPhones are measured up as:

- The iPhone 11 Pro: 71.4 x 144 x 8.1mm
- The iPhone 11: 75.7 x 150.9 x 8.3mm
- The iPhone 11 Pro Max: 77.8 x 158 x 8.1mm

iPhone 11 Pro vs. iPhone 11: Water resistance

The highest IP68 water protection is eligible on all three of the iPhone 11 Pros. iPhone 11 Pro versions can be dipped up to 30 minutes in 6.5 feet deep in water with no adverse consequences. Apple claims you can swim in 4 meters of water for the most luxurious products.

iPhone 11 Pro vs. iPhone 11: Rear cameras

Apple's latest camera set on the iPhone 11 Pro models is becoming a huge deal. iPhone will vary from 0.5x and 2x (ultra wide) into 1x (wide) with a 4x optical zoom in the 11 Pros. A modern Night Mode for highly decreased light functional clicks scene lighting and scene mode. The three phones capture up to 60 fps in 4 K with audio zoom, True Tone light, and Quick Take camera capabilities.

The inexpensive iPhone 11Pro and inexpensive iPhone 11 take ultra-large and small images simultaneously every time you film, and you can then determine which one of them to hold. Return to home electronic fax. Return to the tab from which you come. Home to the sites on which you come. Return to the page you come out of the following Smart HDR generation with enhanced red-eye adjustment with auto image stabilization.

Apple's latest Triple-Camera setup on iPhone 11 Pro devices is a huge surprise, but the iPhone 11 Dual-Camera lens is not a sluggish move:

- Camera I: 12MP wide, f/1.8, OIS
- Camera II: 12MP ultra-wide, f/2.4, 120-degree FOV

iPhone 11 Pro Max and iPhone Pro

- Camera I: 12MP wide, f/1.8, OIS
- Camera II: 12MP telephoto, f/2.0, OIS, 2x optical zoom
- Camera III: 12MP ultra-wide, f/2.4, 120-degree FOV

iPhone 11 Pro vs. iPhone 11: Performance

All Apple's latest A13 Bionic processor supports modern phones that focus machine intelligence. Apple claims the iPhone is also the fastest Processor and GPU.

The upshot, we would predict from all three phones exactly the same excellent results.

iPhone 11 Pro vs. iPhone 11: Biometrics

Apple's new iPhone has a Face ID with 3D face identification, as announced in the iPhone X. This functions the same way, but Apple claims it's 30% quicker, has increased efficiency and greater distance detection.

iPhone 11 Pro vs. iPhone 11: Sound

All of the new iPhones have visual, Dolby Atmos, and 3D video. Current versions for iPhone 11 do include a revolutionary sound visualizer with more realistic 3D audio. The iPhone 11 contains two tiny speakers, not speakers like the Home Pod model.

iPhone 11 Pro vs. iPhone 11: Storage

The Storage rates are the same as mobile phones last year, with each mobile beginning at 64 GB:

- iPhone 11 Pro: 64GB/512GB/256GB
- iPhone 11: 64GB/256GB/128GB
- iPhone 11 Pro Max: 64GB/512GB/256GB

iPhone 11 Pro vs. iPhone 11: Battery/Charging

iPhone 11 Pro versions are extra life-supporting than the iPhone XS, and XR Max claims Apple. All phones have wireless storage, but only the Pro versions have the right 18W charger.

The iPhone 11 is the only handset with a full 18W power adapter, and you may have to purchase one. Apple claims the video playback is up to 20 hours for 11 Pro, and the Standard edition is limited to 18 hours. The XR, XS, and Max earn up to 20 hours each. Here's how Apple describes the life of their phone's battery:

- iPhone 11 Pro: 4 hours extended than iPhone XS
- iPhone 11: 1 hour extended than iPhone XR
- iPhone 11 Pro Max: 5 hours extended than iPhone XS Max

iPhone 11 Pro vs. iPhone 11: Colors

iPhone 11 is accessible in black, red, and silver and yellow. The purple and white pastel tones make their appearance. The iPhone 11 Pro is equipped with a fresh dark green color "midnight" in brown, silver, and gold.

iPhone 11 Pro vs. iPhone 11: Price

Apple shocked everyone that the expense of one of its handsets was significantly cut this year. The price of the iPhone 11 is down to almost $699, and in iPhone XR down to almost $50 $749. iPhone 11 Pro Max and iPhone 11Pro begin almost at $999 and $1,099.

- iPhone 11 Pro: $999/$1,349/$1,149
- iPhone 11: $699/$849/$749

- iPhone 11 Pro Max: $1,099/$1,449/$1,249

1.3 Modern Technology and Usage of iPhone

Apple's first iPhone propelled for the current week ten years back — June 29, 2007. Even though it was not the first gadget whereas hopped path above the market competition and lighted an innovative upset. Scarcely any parts or organizations have been unaltered.

The following are ten insights exhibiting a portion of the main consequences of the iPhone-driven — and Google-driven Android — versatile blast over previous centuries.

1. iPhone has placed the web in everybody's grasp.

As Steve Jobs discharged iPhone just because, he portrayed it as "an advancement cell phone," and "a widescreen iPod with contact control highlights," and an "advancement Web informing device."

Although it is named the iPhone, it is the last part — the Web gadget — which has made the most effective on the earth. This Ericsson chart is generally apparent, indicating versatile voice utilization — moderately consistent development — and extending portable web traffic — advanced by iOS and Android applications, photographs, and, specifically, videos throughout years.

2. iPhone diverted photography, moving it from enthusiasm into a piece of everyday life.

Cell phones, combined with their image altering applications, but not too bad cameras in everybody's grasp, and we have all become enthusiastic picture takers. The fast development of web-based life and other systems administration destinations, in actuality, has offered us an area and a reason to share our pictures.

According to the advertising insight organization KeyPoint Intelligence 1.2 trillion visual pictures taken all around this year, and the more significant part of them—85 percent — will be caught on versatile. That is identical to 400 billion sight and sound pictures gathered in 2011.

3. Apple App Store has changed how applications were created and sold.

Application Store in 2008 was launched by Apple in its with500 applications a year after iPhone was shipped. According to the gadget that supports the user, there are actually 2.1 million in the app store and 3.4 million in Google Mobile Play affiliate. Applications have diverted telephones from a bank to a movement delicate computer game gadget. Undoubtedly, the store of sentimentality could be loaded up with regular items that cell phones supplanted numerous motivations behind routine life, including maps, electric lamps, tickers, scanners, camcorders, schedules, minicomputers, PCs, iPods, and then some.

In the first quarter of 2017, absolute retailer deals for refreshes and in-application exchanges in the Application Store. Google Play rose to $10.5 billion, not considering sales from in-application commercials or administrations.

4. iPhone applications have made a huge difference, including how individuals work.

On-request employments began during the first Web bubble in the late 1990s. As per Steve King, an accomplice at Emergent Research, there was no increase in numbers until the presentation of cell phones with GPS chips and on-request advertising applications. He gathers on-request work information alongside the Intuit charge prep organization.

There are right now around 4,000,000 on-request laborers in the U.S., a figure that is to increase throughout the following four years.

5. iPhones have even altered little things, including gum buys.

Deliberately fixed with magazines in Store checkout lines — and candy for quite some time has been a significant selling point for elastic purchasers. Shoppers remaining in front to pay will look about and make an intuition to buy. Today, however, we are so occupied with our devices that we do not get a sufficient gum sack to fight off our weariness. Regardless, elastic costs have declined by 15% since 2007, the year the iPhone was discharged, as indicated by the showcase examination organization Euro monitor International.

6. iPhones have become our quickest developing fixation — not generally to improve things.

Because of gadgets, individuals invested more energy in watching media a year ago than in recent memory. Socialization, which used to be a non-media marvel, is presently occurring via web-based networking media and portable systems. The time used by individuals on mobile internet browsers has likewise been restricted to other media exercises, such as perusing printed records and staring at the TV.

7. The moving center has changed the notice business — making Google and Facebook the noteworthy champs.

Promotion cash is making a beeline for where the eyeballs are. The web is subbing ordinary media channels like TV for the most showcasing use in the nation. However Internet commercial itself is in transition. Application advertisements utilization is anticipated to overwhelm portable going through this year.

8. iPhone has changed Apple's business — and controlled colossal development.

Apple has delivered $1.9 billion in transactions from $19.3 billion during its 2006 fiscal year, mostly from iPod and Mac. In the ensuing decade, the company has expanded many times. Revenue produced $45.6 billion in sales of $215.6 billion a year earlier. The iPhone made 63% of its sales a year ago — and even a quarter of its income.

9. iPhone has rendered Apple as the best organization on the planet

During the years since the iPhone was launched, Apple came at that point, coming up short. The iPod was a critical advancement motor, yet it was not a lot like what the iPhone would accomplish starting in 2008. At present, Apple's market is more than twice as compared to Exxon Mobile and multiple times better to General Electric, the run of the blue-chip mill portfolio.

10. iPhone has added to the Android people group, improving organizations like Samsung — while murdering BlackBerry while Nokia.

In this modern era, iPhones are in a great deal of lower competition, and incomes from such products are declining. Apple is estimated to deliver 241 million telephones in 2018, comparative with Samsung's 404 million, as indicated by reports from the counseling organization that can accord Genuity. Note that iPhones are expensive as compared to different smartphones with different models, and even though Apple's unit costs are not the most elevated, it's the salary per item.

According to KeyPoint Data, a report with 1.2 trillion views collected during this year, the most critical aspect – 85 percent – is being recorded in a multi-faceted way. It is the same as the 400 billion pictures of sight and hearing recorded in 2011. Apple Store started in 2008 with 500 applications a year after the iPhone was released. The app store currently has 2, 1 million, and the Google Android Play subsidiary has 3, 4 million, according to the user-enabling device. Frameworks also redirected telephones from a bank to a critical machine gadget for travel. Sentimentality shops will certainly be filled with daily products that substituted reasons behind everyday existence, such as charts, electric lights, tickers, scanners, camcorders, calendars, minicomputers, PCs, iPods, and several others.

Chapter 2: iPhone 11 Pro-Specifications, Features, and Functions

New telephones include HDR, a differentiation proportion of 2000, 000:1, and a top brilliance of 800 nits. Right Tone is given to adjust the showcase's white offset with the surrounding lighting in the room, improving things on the eyes, similar to the more extensive tone to render the hues progressively energetic. Apple claims it is made of the hardest glass ever on a cell phone and gives an improved water opposition (IP68) Spatial sound enhancement offers an intuitive listening condition and is bolstered by Dolby Atmos. The principle qualification between iPhone 11 Pro and 12 Max versus the past iPhones is the telephone's triple-focal point structure. The most recent iPhones of Apple incorporate quad, ultra-wide-edge, wide-edge 12-megapixel, and transmitted cameras. The new-age shrewd HDRs are conceivable to perceive objects in the image insightfully. The zooming focal point can ingest 40% all the lighter with a wide f/2.0 gap than iPhone XS Plus with a 2x optical zoom out.

Apple likewise acquainted another Night Mode to take sharp pictures, straightforward and clear in shallow light situations.

The new Deep Fusion highlight, iOS 13.2, utilizes propelled AI strategies for pixel-by-pixel photograph preparing, concealing, detail, and commotion streamlining. The inside comprises of a 7-nanometer A13 Bionic processor combined with a Neural Engine of the third era. The price is $999 for the 11 Pro and $1099 for the greater Pro Max, which is five hours longer than XS Max. Apple markets iPhone 11 pro and Pro Max close by iOS 11, a $699 device that is an iPhone XR's accomplice. It is commonly unclear from the A13 chip, Ultra-Wideband assistance, and various features in Apple's new iPhone 11pro. The A13 is the best portable processor yet, with a 20% expanded CPU and GPU contrasted with A12 — New Machine Accelerators for learning grant the CPU to execute more than 1 trillion trades for each second.

New telephones include HDR, a differentiation proportion of 2000, 000:1, and a top brilliance of 800 nits. Right Tone is given to adjust the showcase's white offset with the surrounding lighting in the room. Price is $999 for the 11 Pro and $1099 for the greater Pro Max, which is five hours longer than XS Max.

Apple markets iPhone 11 pro and Pro Max close by iOS 11, a $699 device that is an iPhone XR's accomplice. It is commonly unclear from the A13 chip, Ultra-Wideband assistance, and various features in Apple's new iPhone 11pro.

The A13 is the best portable processor yet, with a 20% expanded CPU and GPU contrasted with A12—New Machine Accelerators for learning grant the CPU to execute more than 1 trillion trades for each second.

2.1 Design

iPhone 11 Pro and 11 PR Max are equal to XS and XS Max with full-screen OLED screens spreading over 5.8 and 6.5 inches. True Depth camera framework, the front speakers, and different sensors are put one score on the front in any case, besides the meager bezel folding over the edge of every handset. There are normal quiet fastens and volume controls on the left half of iPhone 11 Pro, and on the correct side, you have a side catch that goes about as a control button. Apple assembled a compound steel undercarriage to suit the shade of the body, with practically straightforward radio wire groups above and beneath.

There is no home catch, base bezel, and Contact ID unique mark, with the two models using a BID.

The camera knock is developed of similar glass content as iPhone and falls straight through the client outline, with three focal points set in a triangular type of spotlight and mouthpiece in the area.

All things considered, the three focal points stand up, the two focal points stand up significantly more noticeable than unique XS & Max double focal point camera knock.

iPhone Shades

iPhone XS and XS Max have a lustrous covering, however, Apple utilized a dim completion that feels progressively like cleaned glass on iPhone 11 and 11 Plus.

This year there are four hues: Red, Gray Room, Gold, and Purple Midnight. 12 PM Green is a cutting edge shading that Apple has never utilized, a dull green woodland tint made conceivable by Apple's Seiko Advance ink strategies.

Supportability

iPhone 11 Pro makes of the most broken glass on a gadget, and it will be perfect for unintended skips, drops, wounds, and any slight harm on a basic level. In any case, it is despite everything glass, so it's smarter to utilize an AppleCare+ case in unintended injury.

As per Apple, a "double particle trade cycle" was utilized to fortify the back and front glass to make it stronger than before renditions.

The Obstruction of Water and Cinders

Not at all like the first iPhone XS, iPhone 11 Pro has a water-safe level for IP68 which is completely rough. This has been confirmed to last as long as 30 minutes at a profundity of 4 meters (13 ft.), an update on the XS rating of 2 meters, and a score of 2 meters in the new iPhone 11.

The number 6 in IP68 relates to the residue obstruction (which suggests that iPhone 11 Pro can withstand soil, dust, and different particles), while the number 8 compares to the water opposition. IP6x is the greatest level of residue obstruction usable.

With the IP68 water obstruction mark, iPhone 11 Pro can endure sprinkling, flooding, and brief unintended introduction to water, yet the conscious presentation to water ought to be halted. Apple prompts that water and residue resistance are not irreversible and that customary wear won't break down.

The Apple protection won't make up for fluid mischief to iOS gadgets, and it is savvy to fare thee well while seeing liquids on iPhone 11 Pro.

Sound Room and Dolby Atmosphere

iPhone 11 Pro incorporates a progressive space sound application to mirror the encompassing condition for an increasingly reasonable listening experience. It additionally grasps the enhancement of Dolby Atmos.

2.2 Display

iPhone 11 Pro and 11 Pro Max comprise of an XDR screen with "Super Retina", which Apple claims is their most fantastic exhibition show on an iPhone. Super Retina screen underpins Dolby Vision, HDR10, and a wide assortment of hues for uncommon shading exactness. iPhone 11 Pro with 5.8 "show gives a 2436 x 1125 goal at 458 PPI, while 6.5-inch iPhone11 Pro Max has a 2688 x 1242 goal at 441 PPI. Display Mate: iPhone 11Pro Max has an "altogether more noteworthy introduction than most adversary cell phones" The most up to date screen from Apple is 15 per cent more force successful, prompting striking life of battery enhancements.

Contact Haptic

Haptic Touch is similar to 3D Touch, but not nearly as sensitive. XR iPhone XR users will get the same haptic feedback as the iPhone 6s, but without the need for new technology. Haptic Contact is used with a long press of haptic criticism.

2.3 A13 Bionic Processor

The redesigned A13 Bionic Processor of the following century drives iPhone 11 Pro and Pro Max. A13 Bionic in the past rendition of iPhones is speedier and more impressive than the A12 Bionic Chip, and Apple flaunts it's the best processor at any point utilized in a cell phone.

The two-speed centres in the CPU A13 are up to 20% speedier than the A12 and utilize 30% less fuel, with the four yield centres going up to 20% quicker and utilizing around 40% less fuel.

The A13's GPU is 20% quicker than the A12's GPU and utilizations 40% more fuel.

As indicated by Nanotech research, the A13 offers 50 to 60% better proceeded with the realistic yield on iPhone 11 and 11 Pro than on an iPhone XS and 20 % higher CPU effectiveness.

Processor Functioning

The A13 processor has an 8-centre neural engine of the following decade, which Apple claims are quicker than any time in recent memory for constant imaging and video preparing. A couple of quickening agents for AI empowers CPUs to work up to multiple times faster and consistently creates more than 1 trillion tasks.

The neural motor is supporting up to 20% speedier than the past age of neural motors and requires up to 15 per cent less fuel. Apple claims it controlled the camera arrange, Face ID, AR programming, and Neural Motor.

Center ML 3 for engineers permits the product to use the A13 Bionics' quality for gadgets and sports.

Space for RAM

iPhone 11 Pro and Pro Max appear as though 4 GB RAM for iOS and gadgets, yet it isn't obvious concerning any additional RAM that is committed to the camera as reports have been confounded. We are must sit tight for additional subtleties and see what's inside.

Spilled benchmarks uncovered that the two gadgets had 4 GB of RAM; however, boundaries can be controlled. A Chinese source spill has asserted that there are 6 GB, so it won't be long until we know. iPhone 11 Pro and Pro Max give an interior space of 64, 256, and 512 GB.

2.4 True Depth Camera and Face Id

Apple has presented an improved True Depth camera framework with new equipment on iPhone 11 Pro and Pro Max. Face ID is 30 per cent speedier than before when the application is opened, passwords, and exchanges are encoded. The outline of the face profundity is then moved to the Bionic processor A13, which is placed as a factual function of iPhone used to guarantee the telephone is reached. Face ID utilizes infrared, and it works in low light so night, to ensure that the joined Flood Illuminator implies that a facial sweep is still rendered with satisfactory enlightenment. The implicit Bionic chip A13 guarantees that the Face ID can, after some time, adjust to unobtrusive facial changes so that on the off chance that you develop your hair longer or build up your moustache, it will alter and continue enacting your iPhone.

Wellbeing and Insurance Facial ID

Face ID utilizes a thorough 3D facial output and cannot be deceived by an image, cover, or other guesses of the Face. A "Consideration Aware" confirmation work empowers Face ID to open your gadget just with your eyes open as you face towards an iPhone 11 Pro, so it doesn't actuate. Conversely, your eyes are shut while you rest, when you are snoozing, or when you turn away.

It will be ideal if you note: there is a discretionary availability mode for those incapable of focusing on iPhone screen; however, a great many people will need the extra insurance layer to be permitted.

iPhone 11 Pro perceives when you look at it with the focal point. At the point when considering iPhone 11 Pro, Face ID shows cautions and updates on the Lock screen; it keeps the gadget lit up and right away brings down an alert or ringer when it discovers that you are cognizant that your emphasis is on iPhone 11 Pro show.

Face ID information which is encoded and spared in iPhone 11 Pro Secure an option for Enclave. Neither Apple nor any individual who has your telephone will get to your Face ID information. Confirmation happens exclusively on your PC, without Face ID information spared or transmitted to Apple in the cloud. Outsider engineers have no entrance to the face map utilized by Face ID for getting to a cell phone. True Depth camera can be utilized to check the Face of a shopper and manufacture progressively reasonable Augmented Reality applications.

For Face ID, 1 in 1.000.000 are chances that another person's Face will bamboozle Face ID, however with the substitute appearance revealed in iOS 13, the error chance increments to 1 out of 1 in 500.000. Indistinguishable twins, babies, and a detailed cover have deceived Face ID, yet it is consistently secure enough for the normal resident not to fear in the event that another person will open his iPhone.

Specs of True Depth System

Notwithstanding controlling the Face ID, the True Depth camera framework includes a standard forward-looking camera usually utilized for selfies.

Forward-looking camera in iPhone 11 Pro is updated to 12 megapixels, from 7 megapixels in iPhone XS, supporting Smart HDR for preferred complexity and shading over ever. The new camera will catch 60 fps of 4 K film with 30 fps support for improved picture dynamic range.

At the point when you snap a photo with iPhone 11 Pro, it utilizes a 7-megapixel zoom in the standard representation direction. Transforming your iPhone into scene mode encourages you to get more into the image and make a video of 12 MP2, as do taping the little bolt symbol to zoom out when you are centred around a picture.

For another forward-looking camera, you can abandon representation to scene mode on iPhone 11 Pro to zoom in and in a split second catch more in the image, which is convenient in the conditions like crew vehicles, in any event, when you need to see something behind you in a selfie.

Slofie

The True Depth forward-looking camera can record 120 fps slo-mo recordings just because; permitting a progressive capacity Apple calls "Slofies." These are moderate moving movement recordings indistinguishable from slo-mo camera recordings on past iPhones from the back.

Memoji and Animoji

The True Depth Camera Device bolsters the dynamic, 3D emoticon characters "Animoji" and "Memoji" that you screen with your hands. Animoji is a creature of Emoji type, while Memoji is redone symbols you can assemble.

True Depth examines in excess of 50 muscle movements in various territories of the neck, brow, cheeks, chest, head, jaw, ears, eye, and mouth to permit Animoji and Memoji to work.

All your outward appearances are changed over to the characters Animoji/Memoji, which speaks to your discourse and feeling. In writings and FaceTime applications, Animoji and Memoji can be traded with peers and downloaded.

There are in excess of twelve Animoji, in light of animation characters, which include: rodent, octopus, jackals, giraffe, fish, wolf, warthog, monkey, PC, feline, horse, feathered creature, fox, pig, panda, rabbit, chicken, monster, skeleton, bear, tiger, koala, t-rex, and witch. There is a vast measure of Memoji that you and others will work to resemble. In the Messaging highlight and different pieces of a working framework from iOS 13, non-enlivened Animoji and Memoji stickers can be found.

2.5 Triple-Lens Rear Camera

Triple-Lens Rear Camera iPhone 11 Pro and Pro Max is a triple-focal point back camera, the first on an iPhone. It is the first iPhone with a camera with a zoomed-in lens. The camera application incorporates a committed catch to flip between the three focal points and their shifting central lengths. The three cams can shoot up to multiple times more scenes utilizing their new ultra-wide-edge focal point, ideal for scene pictures, structure photographs, network representations, and that is only the tip of the iceberg.

The camera application incorporates a committed catch to flip between the three focal points and their shifting central lengths with the goal that you can just get the picture you need. The three cams can shoot up to multiple times more scenes utilizing their new ultra-wide-edge focal point, ideal for scene pictures, structure photographs, network representations, and that is only the tip of the iceberg. Apple additionally estimated every sensor independently for white parity, differentiate, and different estimations with the goal that each of the three cameras can work together and go about as one gadget.

The back on the left edge of the iPhone has a focal point and has a 4x centre — this 2x optical zoom in and out, up to 10x advanced zoom.

It has a 120-degree see region and a 12 megapixels focal point for taking close-up pictures and video. It can also take pictures with an advanced ultra-wide-wide camera focal point with 12-megapixels. It is the first iPhone with a camera with a zoomed-in lens. iPhone 11 Pro and 11 Pro Max comprise of an XDR screen with an exceptional camera (Super Retina), which Apple claims are their most fantastic exhibition show on an iPhone. Super Retina screen underpins Dolby Vision and a wide assortment of hues for uncommon shading exactness.

Apple claims it controlled the camera arrange, Face ID, AR programming, and neural motor for the iPhone XS, and claims it's quicker than any time in recent memory for constant imaging and video preparing. The most up to date screen from Apple is 15 per cent more force successful, prompting a striking life of battery enhancements.

Night Mode

With a greater sensor with 100% centre pixels, the full point camera in iPhone 11 Pro empowers, extraordinary failure light usefulness like the Night Mode is intended to take darker pictures with light conditions. It is near the Night Shift highlight of Google, which helps the image utilizing modern AI devices.

The night mode is completely incapacitated in low light circumstances, and the glimmer shouldn't be utilized. On the off chance that you are in a situation of lousy light, the gadget takes a few photographs as the focal point is adjusted by optical signs.

The A13 chip is then used to facilitate pictures for movement adjustment. So frequently, hazy zones are overlooked when more clear pictures combine.

This is accomplished by altering the complexity, adjusting the hues, disposing of pointless clamour, and boosting the clearness to deliver the last picture that shows up a lot more brilliant and crisper as compared to lighting conditions required normally.

The company claims you should play with the Night Mode manual controls to give considerably more detail and less clamour varying so you can see better through the brightening is a long way from ideal.

Picture Design

In iPhone 11 Proforms, representation mode calls for pictures focusing on a subject in the closer view, and the scenery is obscured.

Picture Mode was workable for an iPhone X, however with the presentation of an ultra-wide-ink focal point for profundity recognition, Portrait Mode pictures would now be able to be shot in the current year's iPhone with either fax or a wide-edge focal point.

Representation Mode was confined to a central length in iPhone X, XS, and XS Max. The update causes you to take pictures in representation mode and have a more extensive field of view than beforehand.

The Presence of the Representation

iPhone 11 Pro backings representation lighting, permitting applications to change the brightening impacts of an image. There are distinctive brightening decisions, including Organic, Studio, Contour, Stage, High Key Mono, and Stage Mono.

With iOS 13, Portrait Lighting impacts which can be changed while utilizing a force scale to make progressively unobtrusive looks.

Qualities of the Framework

Apple's Deep Fusion highlight, another picture handling structure using the A13 Bionic and Neural motors, was presented in iOS 13.2. Profound Fusion utilizes complex AI strategies to process pictures pixel by pixel to expand shading, data, and clamour in each piece of the picture. Certain camera decisions incorporate a 36% lighter True Tone light, 63-megapixel scenes twice as enormous, full-shading pictures, live photography help, programmed red-eye amendment and burst highlights.

Abilities for Recording

iPhone 11 Pro and Pro Max show top-quality video on any gadget, Apple says. The fax, wide point, and very wide-edge focal points are working in video mode, so while shooting, you can switch them in them.

iPhone 11 Pro takes 4 K film with the two focal points at 60 edges for every second, and the very long camera records four-fold the number of scenes for more activity pictures.

While recording film up to 60 edges for every second, iPhone 11 Pro backings upgraded dynamic range, and optical picture adjustment is accessible through the normal wide-point camera for video shooting.

A sound zoom is worked to adjust the sound to the image surrounding to permit the account on iPhone increasingly discernible.

Quick Take Easy

Another component called Quick Take lets you get film when you are in photograph mode by holding down the shade, so you can catch a second without progressing from ordinary camera to video mode.

While shooting outside, A13 Bionic will naturally follow a moving subject utilizing the PC during Quick Take mode.

Utilizing Quick Take mode will help swipe option in keeping up video which is longer without the screen button remaining down or swipe left to take a grouping of emotional photographs, which is perfect for activity pictures.

2.6 Battery Life

In the iPhone 11 Pro and Pro Max, Apple records fantastic battery life improvements with A13 Bionic Processor mixed with the new Super (Eye) Retina XDR panel and the updated board power packs. The manufacturer says it's the most excellent battery hop life in an iPhone in modern years. The power is 4 hours greater on iPhone 11pro than on the iPhone XS and the effect on handset 11 Pro Max lasts 5 hours longer as compared to the value on XS Max. The new feature demands for iPhones are constantly met, and the performance is continuously monitored. Apple promises that the product "can have the best possible performance as the battery matures over the years."

Basic Stacking

In just 30 minutes, iPhone 11 Pro and Pro Max will stack half the dead force with a better price. Every new iPhone comes with an 18W USB-C power connector that Apple has recently distributed along with iPads. Apple allows rapid charging on an iPhone only because of the technology.

Charging Broadband

iPhone 11 Pro comprises of a glass body implanted with fused remote charging bows to empower charging remotely. The company uses the Qi remote charging convention utilized even on other Android telephones, inferring that the most recent iPhones will interface with Qi endorsed connector remotely.

iPhone 11 Profits 7.5W and 5W remote connectors; however, 7.5W is speedier downloading. A few organizations have just assembled uniquely made remote charging answers for Apple's iPhones. Numerous 7.5W loaders do not bill 5W on iPhone 11 and 11 Pro supposed to merit recollecting for somebody who wishes to buy a remote charger.

2.7 Connectivity

LTE is better than anyone might have expected on iPhone 11 Pro and 11 Pro Max. Double SIMs work in some specified countries. Apple mixes ultra-broadband and "GPS in the living space," which is assembled unequivocally for better indoor areas.

Apple uses the U1 chip to recognize explicit Apple U1-prepared gadgets effectively, making it harder to locate a missing PC.

The AirDrop function will be presented in iOS 13.1.1, and Bluetooth 5.0 has an increasingly great range, higher paces, network capacity, and expanded interoperability with different remote advances which is discussed in detail below.

LTE Gigabit Class

With the presentation of Gigabit level LTE with 4x4 MIMO and LAA, LTE is better than anyone might have expected on iPhone 11 Pro and 11 Pro Max. 4x4 MIMO and LAA are diverse LTE frameworks that use a few reception apparatuses, different information sources, and an unlicensed range joined with an authorized range to accelerate the LTE as quick as could be expected under the circumstances.

iPhone 11 Pro and Pro Max include progressive iPhone LTE highlights with Gigabit LTE however confined to 2x2 MIMO on a little iPhone 11. Despite the fact that the two most recent iPhones give improved LTE highlights, 5 G isn't empowered and does not work with 5 G systems.

New iPhones permit up to 30 LTE frequencies, which is helpful while flying. Various countries have explicit LTE groups, yet with more LTE band inclusion, iPhone turns out to be bound to be agreeable with close by LTE systems while flying.

Help for double SIM

Double SIM support is remembered for iPhone 11 Pro and Pro Max, empowering double phone numbers to be utilized at once. The double SIM alternative is permitted by including a Nano-SIM space and an eSIM. eSIM in a few countries is available all-inclusive with this Apple gives a definite rundown of transporters offering eSIM on their site. Double SIMs work in some specified countries.

Ultra Wired

iPhone 11 Pro and its models have another U1 chip created by Apple, which permits ultra-wideband space acknowledgement innovation. The chip empowers iPhone 11 to recognize explicit Apple U1-prepared gadgets effectively, making it harder to locate a missing PC.

Apple mixes ultra-broadband and "GPS in the living space," which is exact in light of the fact that it is assembled unequivocally for better indoor areas.

AirDrop means that how Apple uses the U1 chip. Mac expresses that you may rapidly guide your iPhone toward another iPhone, and the PC shows up on your Air Drop objective rundown first. This usefulness will be presented in iOS 13.1.

Wi-Fi and Ethernet

Bluetooth 5.0 forces iPhone 11 Plus. Bluetooth 5.0 has an increasingly great range, higher paces, network capacity, and expanded interoperability with different remote advances.

Bluetooth 5 conveys multiple times the specified network range, volume, and transmits correspondence effectiveness comparative with Bluetooth 4.2. Empowered is Wi-Fi 6 with 2x2 MIMO, regularly known as 802.11ax Wi-Fi. Wi-Fi 6 is the latest Wi-Fi Protocol, which can be gotten to as quick as Wi-Fi 5 (effectively 802.11ac) up to 38%. Wi-Fi 6 is a cutting edge Wi-Fi standard that isn't generally utilized; be that as it may, the assistance throughout the following, not many years are known to be progressively significant.

NFC and GPS

iPhone 11 Pro and Pro Max bolster GPS, GLONASS, Galileo, and QZSS situating administrations.

There is an NFC with per-user mode, and a foundation label choice empowers iPhone models to check NFC labels without the need first to dispatch a gadget.

2.8 Phone Set up, Apps, and Other Features

Congrats! A new iPhone 11, Pro, or Pro Max is your upbeat beneficiary. You will need to dive straight into the telephone when you have the bundle in your pocket, on the whole, take a look and do a touch of arranging! We have a little arrangement direction to which you should pay regard. Of course, it feels like an unnecessary weight, yet it will spare you a great deal of vitality and disturbance. You ought to back up from iCloud, iTunes, or the Finder. Connect your old iPhone to your Pc for a Mobile depiction (macOS Catalina) and discover your iPhone in the Position field to one side. Checking Encrypt nearby reinforcement is a superior alternative on the grounds that your prosperity and information are sponsored up as well – simply pick a secret key that you do not lose. You will recoup your iPhone 11 from the reinforcement after you have marked into your new PC with your Apple ID as you set up the new iPhone 11 following the steps to modify the settings of your phone.

Modify and Remake

That is right; when you get the most recent iPhone 11 under lock and key, you will need to back the current iPhone up in light of the fact that it's as state-of-the-art as could be expected under the circumstances. You ought to back up from iCloud, iTunes, or the Finder.

Connect your old iPhone to your Pc for a Mobile depiction (macOS Catalina) and open another Finder window to discover your iPhone in the Position field to one side. You can see a tab like the iPhone control application in iTunes. Select Save all information on your iPhone to this Mac under the Backups line. Checking Encrypt nearby reinforcement is a superior alternative on the grounds that your prosperity and information are sponsored up as well – simply pick a secret key that you do not lose. Select the Backup tab now.

Catalan macOS iPhone Search

You can discover your iPhone through the Finder in macOS Catalina.

At the point when the reinforcement is finished, connect your new iPhone 11 and afterwards tell your Mac that you need the reinforcement you have recently made.

Prior, in Preferences > iCloud > Backup, you can switch back to iCloud reinforcements. Be that as it may, some of the time, it never helps to run reinforcement on your PC.

For Mac reinforcement (macOS Mojave or more seasoned): the reinforcement strategy is indistinguishable from the one for Catalina referenced above, with the exception of you are utilizing the iTunes programming. iTunes should walk you through the design steps.

Interface PC for iPhone iTunes

For iCloud reinforcement: no association between your old iPhone and your Mac is required. Just beginning Preferences and tap the Apple ID profile page at the left, go to iCloud > iCloud reinforcement and now click Save.

You will recoup your iPhone 11 from the reinforcement after you have marked into your new PC with your Apple ID as you set up the new iPhone 11.

At the point when you get to the Android telephone (Hey, welcome to the nursery!), there is an Android Transfer to iOS programming that will permit you to get to the location, plan. Contacts the entirety of your Google account information, turn over the camera and even move your Chrome bookmarks get to Safari.

Check your old iPhone and afterwards proceed rapidly

iOS has Quick-Start usefulness. It resembles witchcraft. You simply keep your new telephone close to your old telephone and request somewhat to move the entirety of your stuff to the new PC. You will, at that point direct the camera of your old telephone to your new telephone and type the six-digit password of your old telephone.

You will experience the greater part of the arrangement stage, including Face ID, and the telephone is set, much like the old iPhone. You would likewise be approached to reestablish the reinforcement on an old iPhone on the off chance that they are not supported up for some time.

Its product moves the handset through a significant part of the inclinations, home screen arrangement, and that is only the tip of the iceberg. It's a major saver of time. In any case, iOS 11 or later is required, and in the event that you haven't in any capacity whatsoever overhauled your old telephone to iOS 11 (or to the most recent version, iOS 13), perhaps you might want to refresh right away. You would prefer not to hang tight for a critical redesign until your iPhone 11 is close by.

You would need to send it several minutes subsequent to setting up your PC to re-download every one of your gadgets. Your telephone will at first show placeholders of your applications, all assembled and packed into organizers similarly as on your old iPhone. Your most recent iPhone needs to uninstall applications once more, however, as your handset requires an extraordinary version uncommonly intended for this iPhone gadget when you dispatch a thing from the App Store. In any case, record history and inclinations are passed, and that is the basic perspective.

As quick and advantageously, it is consistently basic to back up your telephone, as expressed in a number. When something different turns out badly during the design, you are going to be cheerful you did!

Set up Apple Pay and Face Code

Definitely, for ideal security, Face ID — can be utilized which is the most straightforward approach to get to iPhone 11 is to utilize a complex password that will make it less distressing in light of the fact that you ought not to type it each time.

Setting up face ID is likewise unquestionably more agreeable than contact ID – the design screen can request that you look around a few times. It is a lot simpler to record a unique mark than taping the home catch multiple times.

Face ID design is a lot Simpler than a Touch ID

It is safe to say that you are stressed over your Face ID protection? Try not to be. Try not to be. Neither relinquishes your iPhone with photos of your Face with some other biometric proof — Apple won't get the entirety of this. So that isn't accessible by different gadgets, as various applications do not see your Touch ID fingerprints. You can discover progressively about it in our Face ID FAQ.

Since Face ID is expected to utilize Apple Pay, it is a fantastic chance to jump into the Apple Wallet program for arrangement. At the point when you are new to Apple Pay, simply comply with the bearings for connecting a Visa or two in Wallet. On the off chance that you have had Apple Pay on your old iPhone as of now, you will discover the Visas on the current iPhone lapsed. Why? Why? Normally, for your wellbeing. There will be a wallet history; however, many Master cards you would like to use for Apple Pay would need to be reemerged.

Overhaul your Product

Great, you will, finally, be on your most recent iPhone on your home screen. Visit the App Store first — you would need the entirety of the applications to have the most recent forms. Quest for refreshes, open the App Store program and afterwards press the upper right of your record symbol. An alarm include is open, and you can get the cautions here.

Remember to auto-update your applications by changing updates to Settings > Apple ID > iTunes and App Stores. Else, you can physically refresh the product and just check the discharge takes note of "What's new" to perceive what has improved.

Pair the Watch with Apple

You should join it with your new iPhone to keep the action information streaming into your wellbeing database and keep your notification streaming into the watch on the off chance that you utilize an Apple Watch.

Start the Apple Watch application with your new iPhone 11, which will take you through blending, including password settings, opening conduct, and Apple Pay.

In the event that you do not as of now run your Apple Watch, you will need to refresh it. Apple Watch requires to be associated with the iPhone.

At that point look for iPhone Watch programming update choice. Apple Watch update can be a long activity, which settles on it a keen decision to begin early.

Peruse among Various Activities and Requests

As it is normally thought of, there is no home catch on your iPhone 11. On the spot of the home catch; presently you have a glorious OLED see with an extra half-inch or somewhere in the vicinity!

Regardless of whether you are utilizing an iPhone X or XS, it will presumably be recognizable. However, you have some new developments to know whether you change from a more established iPhone.

The following are a couple of basic orders to relearn since your iPhone is "away from home".

Return Home: Immediately move the base of the gadget away. Basic! Straightforward!

Spring between Telephones: Spring left or directly down the screen to snap between gadgets. You can channel "flick" from the base corners, move your finger to and fro and "ricochet" through your telephones, or basically slide one next to the other.

Gadget switch: Swipe from the base and defer a second on the show with your key. Gadget cards come up rapidly so you can take up your finger, so tap it around.

Close a gadget: Just snap on in the event that you have to incapacitate a thing from the gadget turn.

Take a screen capture: simply press the side catch and the volume button simultaneously.

Look for Photograph Lighting

You as of now learn Portrait Mode in the camera application in the event that you update from a Plus-Model iPhone. Albeit even iPhone 8 Plus, X, and XS had Portrait Illumination, which is likewise on iPhone 11, obviously. Just begin the camera application, pick representation from the camera modes on the base of the gadget, and afterwards flip the various decisions of lighting.

Photograph Lighting will convey your picture photographs on the following stage on your iPhone 11.

iPhone X propelled Portrait Mode on the forward-looking camera, and it'll be another component for you on iPhone 11 when you update from it.

There is some defence for the new iPhone 11 to have that polished glass back, not on the grounds that it is vengeance against your iPhone 4. Truly, this glass back permits remote stockpiling. To utilize this element, you should have a perfect remote charge cushion utilizing the Qi standard. What you will do is place your iPhone on the cushion and watch it keep on driving up on the off chance that you have one of those lying around. Advise goodbye to the bedside table's mix of Lightning links!

Normally, on the off chance that you like your iPhone 11 can be stacked through Lightning. It is the least demanding approach to charge your gadgets in the event that you utilize the right fitting and string.

The 11 can be accused rapidly of the USB-C Power Delivery (USB-PD) model. Apple has a battery converter of 18 watts, regardless of whether you have an iPhone 11 Pro or 11 Pro Max. Tragically, iPhone 11 force connector is a 5-watt assortment. You will utilize the USB-C power connector for 29 Watts or the USB-C power connector for the exemplary MacBook Pro. Yet, USB-C power connectors from outsiders will work just as the USB-PD model. We have checked all the affirmed Apple power connectors and chose outsiders and find that the 12-watt iPad connector is the perf.

Chapter 3: Consumer Reviews and Availability

On the off chance that you effectively own an iPhone XS, XS Max, or even an XR, you can most likely set aside your cash and pause. Enormous bounces in battery life and new cameras aside, there could very well not be sufficient in the method of new highlights to legitimize burning through $1,000 or more on a different telephone.

If you are prepared for a redesign, however, these telephones are high-performing, smooth machines. What is more, on the off chance that you need to spare some scratch, remember the $700 iPhone 11. Select one of those, and you pass up an OLED show, a 2X back camera, and a superfast charger alongside crazy long battery life.

Likewise, we cannot underscore enough how close the scoring is at the head of our cell phone evaluations. In certain classes, just portions of a point separate the top models.

In the meantime, remember 5G is coming. iPhones good with these superfast systems are generally expected to dispatch one year from now. A few people should pause and futureproof their next telephone buy.

Be cautioned, however: If Apple follows the case of Samsung, which began selling 5G telephones this year, those iPhones will be the absolute priciest available. You may be forced to put back the cash and pause whether you have an iPhone 11, 11 pro or 11 pro Max. Huge improvements in battery life and improved sensors may not be enough to legitimize burning over $1,000 or more on a particular handset by way of fresh highlights. Nonetheless, these telephones are high-performance, quiet devices until you are ready for an overhaul.

3.1 Consumer Verdict by Apple and the Benefits Associated

Following a slip up a year ago, Apple is back on top with what is just the best littler telephone accessible. iPhone 11 Pro has longer battery life, a superior screen, and incredible presentation all round.

The camera is likewise a significant improvement in transparency and execution, especially in fine detail and little light, with the additional night mode currently coordinating opponents. It won't yet substitute an advanced SLR for my expert photography. However, it's nearer than anything there has been previously.

The plan is as yet a victor at this size, yet is beginning to look a little dated three years on from the shape breaking iPhone X. What is more, there is not a single 5G to be seen either when we're directly on its cusp being a key differentiator for 2020.

It's not great, yet in the ocean of ever-bigger, hand-extending telephones, it's reviving to have a relatively simple model to pocket, hold and utilize one-gave that doesn't settle on force or highlights.

The most significant issue with iPhone11 Pro is its cost. The beginning expense of £1,049 accompanies just 64GB of capacity, which means you will probably need to depend vigorously on distributed storage on the off chance that you shoot countless photographs, recordings, or download applications or films.

It would not be considered that iPhone 11 Pro is even distantly acceptable worth since it is most certainly not.]For £1,049 and up, you are purchasing a single item at this size and following through on a substantial premium cost for the benefit.

Apple iPhone 11 Pro has IP68 dust/water safe (up to 4m for 30 mins), It offers Apple Pay (Visa, MasterCard, AMEX affirmed), It presents an amplifier, with sound system speakers, and it has dynamic clamour abrogation with devoted mic. It has models, for example, A2215, A2160, and A2217, its cost is around 1150 EUR. It accompanies a glimmer that empowers you to take astonishing photographs in low light conditions. It offers a non-removable Li-Ion 3190 mAh battery that goes on for quite a while. It contains GPS, with A-GPS, GLONASS, GALILEO, QZSS, and NFC highlight to move information.

Of starters, Wi-Fi, Ethernet, Wi-Fi, USB, 3 G and 4 G, Apple iPhone 11 Pro offers lovely battery limitations. Face ID ensures improved mobile protection, with excellent cameras and a wide variety of highlights. It provides great polls and a smaller usage of resources. This delivers innovative, cutting-edge technology, excellent imagery. This does not have Infrared; it doesn't have expandable memory with the card release, it is 188 g (6.63 oz.) large item

3.2 User Reviews

IPhone11 Pro is Apple's most recent iPhone with individuals asking what is truly changed. It is a reasonable inquiry since it looks fundamentally the same as an iPhone year before. Be that as it may, utilize the new cameras for a couple of moments, and both that question and curious looks from sceptics rapidly blur.

• The standard iPhone 11 offers incredible double cameras, yet iPhone11 Pro provides a third camera for optical zoom, giving you more range.

- Apple's new Night mode produces astounding outcomes in little light and even outperforms the Pixel 4 sometimes.

- The broadened dynamic range in video and realistic adjustment produces a film like outcomes.

- Thanks to its A13 Bionic processor, iPhone11 Pro is the quickest telephone you can purchase.

- At about 10.5 long periods of battery life, iPhone11 Pro offers great continuance; however, iPhone11 Pro Max endures almost 12 hours on a charge.

- Nevertheless, consider the $700 iPhone 11 pro because you have little risk of getting hit.
- Pick one and take an OLED display, a 2X rear camera and a super-fast charger along with an insanely long battery life.
- Similarly, we cannot adequately stress how similar the performance is to our cellular assessments.
- For certain groups, the top models are only divided by portions of a stage.
- Meanwhile, note the 5 G arrives. Better iPhones with such superfast systems should usually be deployed from now on for one year.

- Most citizens will stop to purchase their new phone for the future.
- Be warned, though, that if Apple follows the example of Samsung, which this year began offering 5 G products, such iPhones would be the absolute size.
- After a fall a year ago, Apple is back on top of what is the best open handset. iPhone 11 Pro has longer battery life, excellent processor and incredible show all around.
- The camera also significantly improves clarity and performance, particularly in fine detail and in low light, with the additional night mode currently organizing opposing players.
- It will not substitute professional photography with an advanced SLR yet.
- The strategy is indeed a success but begins looking a little close to three years after the iPhone X breakup. In fact, there is no 5 G to be found as we are a primary differentiator immediately at its cusp for 2020.
- It is not perfect, and yet it's revitalizing in the ocean of ever-larger, hand-extending phones to get a fairly basic layout that doesn't depend on power or spotlight.

3.3 Pricing and Warranty

iPhone11 Pro is currently discounted (Sept. 20). It begins at $999 ($41.62 every month) for a generally tiny 64GB of capacity. With an exchange, iPhone11 Pro can be had for as meagre as $599 at Apple on the rear chance that you have an iPhone XS in excellent condition. The Galaxy Note ten packs fourfold the amount of capacity at 256GB. There is a one year guarantee accessible for iPhone bought and gave by the permit under the organization.

3.4 Availability and Other Related Products

iPhone 11 master is accessible worldwide under the pennant of approved suppliers of the organization including

- AT AND T
- SPRINT
- T MOBILE
- VERIZON

These telephones are provided to the transporters and afterwards are conveyed worldwide to the suppliers and various distributors in telephone markets in different corners of the world.

What is in the Box?

This time around, Apple's retail box adornments for iPhone11 Pro and Pro Max are very not entirely the same as the ones that transported with their immediate ancestors. While the iPhones XS dispatched with a USB-to-lightning link, lightning Ear Pods, and a 5W connector, Apple has made significant and long past due to overhauls with the retail box substance of iPhone11 Pro and iPhone 11 Pro Max.

IPhone11 Pro and Pro Max have become Apple's first cell phones to deliver with an 18W USB-C power connector and lightning to USB-C link. These, notwithstanding the real gadget and lightning Ear Pods, raise the check of the cell phones' retail box substance to five when we also incorporate the documentation.

The 18W connector will demonstrate a boon to a ton of clients as they won't need to make the separate acquisition of the frill any longer. Moreover, the USB-to-lightning link will guarantee that the iPhones 11 Pro can without much of a stretch interface with the present note pads and PCs. Apple's settled on a decent choice this year, though later than it ought to have.

The iPhones 11 Pro and Pro Max will be up for pre-request on Friday at 9 are PDT, and the gadgets begin transporting on the Sept. 20. They have a $999 beginning sticker price and come in 64GB, 256GB, and 512GB capacity designs.

Apple Pay Method

Provide your App Store, iTunes Store, iCloud installation info. When you modify the update info, it is updated for all software and management for the Apple ID. The deployment methods you have on the database will be removed from your iOS 12.1.x or before and alter the billing or shipment installation techniques. You cannot adjust the question that this process charges the Apple ID balance. You cannot change the balance paid to your Apple ID via Apple Pay. To get the same sum of money back, you must adjust the price paid with each purchase. You need to adjust the balance that is paid with each fee that is paid for the entire price you pay for the ability to use Apple Pay. You cannot adjust the price for each shopping to the sum you create using iTunes, or other third-party applications use Apple Pay to clear the balance. The price you pay for these apps and facilities is paid by Apple Pay.

Chapter 4: Challenges Faced by Emerging iOS 13 Technology

When it is considered iOS 13 is finally ensured, along with this comes iOS 13.5. Due to this, the company had been increasing some high ground with versatile Operating Systems. Notwithstanding temperamental rollout, things seem to move backward concerning the available version of O.S. for iPhone. Every subsection of this chapter portion discusses the most conspicuous problems faced in each type of the Operating System and any philosophies that should be considered.

With the origination of iPhone and Apple products, the emerging technology introduced by Apple has changed immensely. It started to vary a great range of its operating system from simple IOS to the latest update of IOS 13. Where the technology was significantly emerging and developing itself, it faced several issues also which were handled by the later updates. But for the users who have not upgraded their system subsequently, there are some temporary solutions to the problems faced by several iOS.

In this chapter are discussed the problems faced by later to former IOS 13 introduced in the market.

This is also simpler to visit the App Store and discover, read about, and purchase fresh smartphone devices. The smartphone software supports the current iPhone 8 Plus and iPhone X Portrait Lighting feature. From early 2018, you will be able to use the Messaging feature to transfer cash to others immediately and safely. Check out the latest device group, A.R. Devices, to find out if you have an increased truth. The control center continues to have easy access to standard functions of the iOS 11, such as Airplane, Wi-Fi, and Bluetooth, which can be activated and turned off. The App Store software offers you internet exposure on your iPhone or iPad to over two million applications. You will discover techniques for utilizing each of these apps in the book later.

What's more, remembering that not related to a specific iOS update, Apple, a large portion of a month earlier, perceived a veritable programming shortcoming in iOS 13 working by utilizing the default section for mails on iPhone. The security organizations responsible for cybersecurity has so far reported a zero-click misuse, which implies customers do not adequately misuse it since it's assessed remotely. Several models of iPhone with running iOS systems seem to be spammed by such cyber-attacks.

Therefore due to update, those onwards six have fixed the flaws in any occasion for smartphones that helps iOS 13. Some other actions taken by the organization include change out of Mail by Apple and Gmail or some other mail program.

Following months in beta, Apple launched iOS 13 in September 2019. After the day of its transmission, there have been more concerns and problems than expected. Here are several typical iOS 13 focal points and what you should do to repair them, beginning with the new definition. It's by no way an intense one-on-one, so it's a starting point for anyone seeking to address the big problems.

4.1 Get ready for 13.5.5 and 13.5.1

The company has released beta versions of iOS 13.5.5, including all the reserves of being based on bug pounding. Besides the bug pounding, no more features are introduced, a single security update, and appallingly no fixes for bugs in the system. With these, there are some glitches in face id, background, Bluetooth accessibility, garage band application, which stop working suddenly. Complaints to @ apple support have recorded screen catches of this miracle. It will likely dispatch another audio fragment to the apple news+ electronic participation organization Macintosh.

The common errors faced by iOS 13.5.5 and 13.5.1 are jailbreaking of gadgets and associability issues faced due to coronavirus in the globe the new update consists of nothing more than the fixation of these small glitches. It also fixed Bluetooth associability and garage band application, which stopped working all of a sudden.

Apple released iOS 13.5.1 on May 20. The update fixes a shortcoming of the starting late release uncovering jailbreaking gadget and goes after every progression type of iOS. New features include nearby assistance for the structure of coronavirus helplines contact-following applications with some organizations. Facial id recollects that whether the user wears a face shroud subsequently results in better use of group FaceTime.

Mp4/mpeg-4 playback of encoded content does not go after individual phones. iPhone Organizer Company has subsequently worked on fixing any shortcoming that makes it easier for users to connect with iOS 13.5. The company has not said what it plans to do about the bug. The bug could open a couple of customers to advanced attacks.

4.2 New in iOS 13.4 and 13.4.1

Improvements have been introduced by iOS 13.4.4 in Mail applications comprising of toolbar upgrade and encryption systems. Memoji sticker includes several new choices which made the presentation of stickers, with broad purchase support for the App Store. Starting late-play arcade games, you directly appear in the Arcade tab, so there is a continuous working on all stages. iPad OS 13.3.1 update showed up on April 7 with a couple of bug fixes. FaceTime issues were fixed, which summons the components that do not chip at earlier variations of iOS. In mail applications with toolbar enhancements and security schemes, iOS 13.4.4 has been released with updates to launch delayed play in arcade games. Another 13.3.1 upgrade concentrated on correcting glitches about delayed updating of iOS 11 and 11 pro images. It operated on addressing the pictures and exchange problems via mail, which is frequently encountered while using the camera when utilizing FaceTime.

The company released iOS 13.3.1 as the most recent version of the working of a compact structure.

This update passes on fixating the issues found in previous updates, including squashes bugs and lifts execution functions. If you do not get a modified notification or upgrade genuinely after updating the iPhone with a new update for the iPhone 6 originally and later versions yet, select Settings open General and arrive at Software Update option. It will download total updates from ongoing interpretations starting now opted on your device.

IOS 13.3.1 fixes Communications bugs in which users have boundless authority. It causes the issue when youngsters can call or use FaceTime or visit and send messages to their friends and family without any protected access. New update in the same manner as the previous ones handle the same issue by surrendering most to date released iPhone models such as in iPhone11 game plan the ability to cripple Ultra-Wideband through another flip switch. This thrashing is the matter of the region you opted when the contraption's territory organizations were flipped off, which company blamed on its Ultra-Wide chip for Band.

Extra 13.3.1 updates focus on fixing bugs concerning iPhone 11 and 11 pro pictures modifying with delay; it worked to fix the pictures and trade issues while using mail, a camera error that is often observed while using FaceTime.

The update also fixes message pop-ups upon the Wi-Fi button and handles deformed Sound in Car Play options while manufacturing attachment ports of specific vehicles.

4.3 New iOS 13.3.1 issues

In the recent update, there have been several issues detected concerning complaints with respect to interface slack, application issues for nearby and outcast applications, Airplay, Touch and Face ID issues, and battery channel. When issues like freeze and crash in Exchange of Home Pod, Bluetooth, Wi-Fi, and Car Play are detected, which guarantee there is free space in iPhone to present update, and not surprisingly, make a point to back up your data before starting.

In 13.1 iOS interface slack, application issues for nearby and outcast applications, Airplay, Touch and Face ID issues, and battery channel. When issues like freeze and crash in Exchange of Home Pod, Bluetooth, Wi-Fi, and Car Play were detected update was introduced and fixed in 13.5.

The new iOS 13.4 update will most likely have new features. There is no official release date as of not long ago; those inside tracks foresee it will be eventually in March. The update is 200MB for a spot update from 13.3.

4.4 New in iOS 13.3

IOS 13.3 gives guards more authority over children's online correspondences inside Screen Time highlight. Gmail, Dropbox, Twitter, Outlook, and Facebook all help security keys. Update in like way gives new game plans in Apple News+ stories. The new iOS structure does not fix the Ultra-Wideband and zone sharing issue. With iOS 13.3, there were several functioning errors with mobile data, communication limitation, and iPhone used by kids and other security purposes along with the error in battery channel and wireless charging port.

Mobile data

Many consumers point by point have lost their adaptable cell structure along with the IOS 13.3 base. Others have also claimed that their Wi-Fi signals have been disabled and cannot write or call traditional messages. Apple support fuses for these kinds of messages: My iPhone 7 Plus' web affiliations have been broken from the past Sunrise, and it can even get warnings, so it can say, when you open the app, that I do not get a web affiliation, either via adaptable information or Wi-Fi. IOS 13.3 is running. Apple has proposed different proposals.

For fixing such errors, the user should go in Settings pick Airplane mode and allow and disable it. Adjust Settings for System open General Click Reboot. When asked, enter your secret key. Certify that the factory settings must be changed. If you agree, your system can restart uninstall all installed Wi-Fi frames and Bluetooth synchronized contraptions, cell frames, and VPNs to restore the original factory setup. Push your iPhone to restart or reset if you're not using the strategies below to utilize easy data accompanying your iPhone. Keep and click the side grab and volume before the slider begins to come up. Move the joystick to operate the iPhone. Keep on gripping and clicking (on the right screen) the screen pick before the Apple logo shows up.

Communications Limitation prohibits kids from talking with anyone.

The 13.3 Standards on messaging require guards to monitor whom their teenagers might phone, email, or FaceTime. Apple says that the problem only happens when a "non-standard arrangement" is set up, Apple Watch, along with Siri will be able to text or call anyone with the requests regardless of whether they are on the contact list. The flaw does not work for Twitter, Snapchat, and Skype on WhatsApp.

Push iCloud accounts to synchronize as normal. Use it from other settings in iCloud — default, Gmail, or anything other than what you expect.

Battery channel

The controlled battery in iOS 13.3 does not present another question — it is an established problem that never vanished. One user says on Twitter: "My iPhone 7 is practically resuscitated to iOS13.3. Battery life is so far linked to now. Calculate how we will continue now with our lives." Battery life problems are a challenge with the iOS revives. We noticed that when iOS 13 was first updated, although the situation was not significantly modified for anyone. Many iOS 13 users have found the battery life has been destroyed with Apple's new robust operating climate. This is usually because the latest O.S.O.S. would provide distinctive logistical functions to integrate with the contraptions, including Spotlight, Photos, and a variety of iCloud jobs.

With iOS 13 and later, you can relive applications by opening your account in the App Store and then clicking recently updated. Low demand limits iPhone production and the ability to use battery energy. IOS Update licenses programs well out without manual knowledge to stay robust.

Of great magnificence, power capacity can be shortened, and a boost to battery life will be given in iOS 13. It takes just a few hours for all to return to normal, particularly when your computer recovers generous iCloud volumes or changes data from several sources. The after upgrading your phone icon of the better battery in your iPhone menu bar turns yellow with which you can start working again. Battery life on an iPhone or iPad will take up to two days when the device is reopened, and the computer is turned off for a lengthy time. The iPhone screen will be dark if the light of the device is too long to function.

4.5 iOS 13.2 and iOS 13.1.3

IOS 13.2 passed on several new highlights, including Deep Fusion camera tech on iPhone 11 and later structures. Announce Messages with Siri choice let Siri read pushing toward messages so anyone may hear while you had Air Pods related with your ears.

Different updates included listening history for the Music application, improved Siri and Dictation that let you quit allowing records to Apple.

Macintosh discharged iOS 13.1.3 and iPad OS 13.3 with other bug fixes and execution upgrades for all gadgets to address issues in the Mail application, Bluetooth availability, and dispatch execution for Game Center applications, among other things. The update was proposed to manage Bluetooth issues, for instance, by isolating on explicit vehicles, comparatively improving steady quality for smaller hearing partners and headsets. It fixed an issue that could forestall blending in with or getting alarms on an Apple Watch. For the updated versions of 13.2 and 13.1.3, the issue of Siri making a call by itself, apple pay, Bluetooth, dropped contacts, and loss of contacts was faced by users for which the recovery and connectivity solutions.

Siri makes approaches speakerphone according to ordinary methodology.

Apple's social gatherings have revealed a few issues with Siri while making calls. Since reestablishing to iOS 13, it is observed that Siri approach to make a call for the user, the call is set using speakerphone each time, and Siri commonly does this.

This is not known as self-referencing, but the Siri set to put the speaker on itself and start to make calls to the person of its choice.

Each time something like this is experienced, "Welcome, Siri, call Jim." The call is placed and put on speakerphone. By this time, it can be handled by turning talk time off and later on restarting the phone. This is especially serious if you're driving. Here is a workaround that may work subordinate upon your iPhone model:

For resolving this issue, click Availability, open Touch click on Call Audio Routing, and associate through Bluetooth Headset. On the off chance that you brief Siri by tapping the force button, this methodology may work correspondingly, yet it combines your hands, leaving the issue to make sense of to you that how to utilize telephone while driving.

Cannot set up Apple Pay in iOS version 13.2.2

Despite the way that iOS 13.2.2 has streamlined different bugs, a few clients kept revealing more different issues. For instance, unable to set up Apple Pay a great deal in the wake of resetting the entirety of the settings in iOS 13.2.2. An iPhone 7 client reported it. As the speediest procedure to teach this issue to experts asked to run a power reboot.

If a power restart doesn't work for it, the customer should log out of Apple ID and connect it back again.

Where this option also does not work, it is suggested to reset the region:

Select Setting open Name at that point reach iTunes and finally, App Store, click Apple ID, and a brief timeframe later View Apple ID. Pick a Country or Region to transform it.

Bluetooth issues in iOS 13.2.2, 13.1.3

Bluetooth of the iPhone does not interface other Bluetooth contraptions of your telephone.

Attempt to exchange the Airplane mode out and turn off and, from that point, change the structure settings. Select Settings by then open General select Reset and open Reset Network Settings to escape the spared settings, VPN settings, Wi-Fi passwords, and upheld systems.

Restart to fix the iOS framework to reestablish the entire Bluetooth mastermind.

Dropped signals in iOS 3.1.3 and 13.1.2

Apple's iOS 13.1.2 made calls drop inside a delineation of being set. The call will be dropped following 30 seconds to a second. Calls from some distant applications likely would cause the error concerning understanding from the other side. For updates of iOS 131.3, 13.2.2, and 13.3, which often show it out of reach, try resetting network settings or VPN settings with bolstered systems and Wi-Fi passwords.

Dropping calls more often after the user has experienced iOS 13 updates. A wide margin shocking after 13.1.2 update is also experienced. It uses the telephone for the business, not as the best purpose to use one customer commented on apple's twitter support system site. While some customers commented, everything is extraordinary right now with the update, and no glitches are experienced while making calls. Some said they had a relative issue until they reinforced their phone and did a full factory restore with the latest iOS, after which phone is working perfectly from being connected back to mail and online at home servers. Going back to the page you came from. The user can still make calls using apple's iPhone 6, 7, 8, and 9-month-old iPhone 5 and the iPhone 5s update placed by the company.

Lost contacts in iOS 13.1.3

During the revival of iOS 13.1.3, many iPhone customers learn about their separating Contacts application. Many of them have reference names, but no substance in them, while others are practically unfulfilled. This question illustrates the value of protecting the mobile.

ICloud sharing connection option uses iCloud to recover any or a touch of your connections without overwriting current knowledge.

Select Open Your Name Preferences, click on the Contacts iCloud button. When it's off, turn Contacts on, then you may pick your gadget to launch late coordinated contacts. Decide to hold them on Merge with iOS. Your data will be recovered.

Re-sync your iCloud contacts; use the default for iCloud at this stage. Tap Open Contact Settings Select Standard Account and link to iCloud. Reset all settings by syncing iCloud contacts at that stage. Reset your iPhone and restore your iTunes at the stage you see errors. Then sign up to iCloud and then synchronize your numbers. Choose Contacts press Community and then open Search iCloud to view the entire contacts. Reset the device for better performance.

4.6 iOS 13 issues originally

Above all, the basic issue faced by iOS 13, which pertained in all its updates were concerning mail, connectivity, reminder sync, and third-party interference. The company overlooked these issues, and all the glitches were overcome slowly with the evolution of new updates being introduced timely.

Apple Mail

Various things with iOS 13 Mail execution were addressed. iPhone does not allow alternatives, such as not submit texts. It simply opens up a non-ending framework draft. It fails to stack email and untouchable mail accounts. It fails to permit new documents, it does not work because there is no sender problem where you cannot tell who sent them.

One client who contributed to the company's official site: "Not choosing to see which source is obvious." In this case, when you click the button recipient bar seems to appear empty. Therefore you cannot do anything in this respect. In some cases, the email also delivers a double email to recipients contrary to sending an empty mail.

There are various responses to an extremely boisterous mail program in iOS 13, which are responsive to what you encounter. Below are a variety of problems and approaches surrounding brokenness in mail applications?

Thanks to system revive, you can validate for disconnected programs, such as Gmail and Yahoo Mail, which you applied to mail through searching the Application Store.

In case the mail options do not function, guarantee that the mail application is allowed. Tap the Mail button on Notifications and then press Activate Notification. Dispatch Settings.

You should create more than one email address; seek to remove limitations preventing you from user accounts. This is done by Dispatch settings for this click Screen Time from this stage and Choose Content and Privacy Restrictions. Open allowed applications and enter the mail by clicking the click button. This helps you to merge various documents through the mail station program.

Engage mail program with settings for cellular details, and then move to Mail collection at the cellular.

You will go to open General Snap Reset and tap Reset Network Configuration Settings for resetting network settings. To continue, your password is needed.

Test the Options Move or Pick and Optimizing Account Manual Choices to optimize the use of Flexible Settings by tapping on Login and Account settings and then tap Fetch New System Settings.

Power should be stopped and restored to the mail application. It is a prominent methodology when mail does not fitly synchronize. Tap the House Click twice to show each running code, push it to the top to shut it, and start it again.

If you're unlikely to pump iPhone mail demand, restart your computer.

If anything that fails, delete the mail client from your computer and reconnect it again. At that level, tap Settings and enable Passwords by tapping account. The mail records are displayed on the screen. Select the record of choice at that point, snap it. Disable Account Option should show at the base of the computer. Click to delete the system log. Set it up again by then.

Connectivity problems with Application Store

For Wi-Fi and iOS 13 cells, there have been various design concerns. The Twitter support site of Apple leaves a message which concerns the use of the phone in the App Store. It normally didn't work on iOS 13, 13.1, and 13.1.1. We will hold it continually reinforced enough to bring it to function. Connection issues will enter a pre-packaged program where you cannot connect with the iTunes Store when attempting to deploy the iOS, App Store, or Apple Books. Now and again, the app won't load anything or wait for a request.

Apple provided two or three tips on the best possible way of fixing a cell alliance problem for the Apple Books, Application Store, and iTunes.

Test configuration arrangement agreements that contract and guarantee this on the network and its associated software.

Using the application and connecting with any platform and pledge, it will bring lots on the extraordinary event that you do not try to configure any contraction on a virtually identical device.

When you are not willing to use the cell company to communicate with your contracting page, ensure that your mobile data is turned on for the iTunes, Application Store, and Apple Books. This can be turned on by going to Mobile Settings, then pressing cellular, and entering Cellular Information.

With the unusual option that you cannot log in to your Apple ID, reset your I.DI.D password.

If closer to checking the portion information, ensure that the portion strategy, the charge address, and the name are correct.

Select Settings reach general and open date and time, then switch on automatic mode. Open Settings reach general and open date and time.

Reminders Sync

With iOS 13, they are providing another interface to the reminder with new features, records, and some abundant toolbar options having the ability to merge web links, images, and stories. In any case, a few customers report issues with developing missing records, removed animates, notes, names along with the list all resetting to default with wrong time and date, along with the arrangement of different issues on official apple support accounts customers have mentioned: "If it's indistinguishable to you fix stimulates starting at now." It is a finished bunch. You haven't had the decision to get the chance to resuscitate since energizing to iOS 13.

Apple saw that reminders wouldn't encourage fittingly except if your contraptions ran the latest programming, including mac. According to the company, "upgraded resuscitates are not acceptable with changes of iOS and macOS. On the magnificent chance that you upgrade your reports on iPhone with iOS 13, iPad and mac utilizing the equivalent iCloud account cannot get to refreshes until iPadOS and macOS 10.15. According to apple, you will have the choice to get regular reminders on icloud.com, which will subsequently help clients running iOS 13 to surrender a complete reminder schedule until macOS Catalina is recovered. With this technique, clients can avoid reminders issues.

It is connecting the device to the web before opening the reminders application considering the method to open it in the wake of the procedure provided to strengthen iOS 13.

To activate the application, a welcome to reminders screen appears to offer an option to refresh the application later or right now to the user. Updates will relatively give you information about reminders, records, or diverse shared contraptions, which must be an overhaul.

Click upgrade now or later; the application's screen has a button for upgrade accessible. It can be clicked at the time user chooses to invigorate. It helps redesign impacts existing updates in major iCloud accounts, yet not those in other iCloud, CalDAV, or exchange accounts. Organizations work beside the alarm option than sharing a reminder list will help add people to the network, which does not work in iOS 13. In contrast, the association guarantees further to handle the issue in a future update.

Third-party Interference

The company gave excellent safety warnings regarding unapproachable iOS 13 help applications. For instance, Gboard or SwiftKey, or many others, can run pariah as free applications.

Full OS access is requested to connect to different gadget applications to give additional highlights.

It concerns merely consoles in this category which have complete access to the system, and mean that the business has collaborated with consoles or other calm devices that do not need maximum access and are not impacted. The device builders will get keystroke details with complete control. In addition to this full exposure on gboard, you will see Gmail directly from the compensation submitted to Gmail.

System upgraded, to iOS 13.1.1 or iPad OS 13.1.1, to address issues concerning the iPhone, iPad, or iPod contact's unapproachable consoles. Ensure that complete access without your permission or agreement is permissible and keep down settings by pressing general on the keyboard tap and opening keyboards. You should not trust remote consoles to uninstall.

Chapter 5: Additional Tips and Tricks to Use iPhone 11 Pro

IOS 13 accompanies several highlights include the renditions of previous highlights, whether have iPhone 11 or 11 pro accompanying the new updates along with. The same tips work for those having Iphone old versions of iPhone with running iOS 13 efficiently these phones there are a significant number of highlights and relevant tips despite the fact these apply. In a brief overlook, this chapter mainly focuses on following key points concerning the techniques and tips provided by experts under the technical support team by Apple and other software developers

To manage any glitch occurring due to the update of iOS in your iPhone 11 pro, you must initially restart it by pressing the power button and letting it hold on for few minutes.

This approach usually helps in case it does not work. There are several alternative tips and techniques discussed in chapter considering in the context of all subheadings.

5.1 Safari and iCloud Tips

DuckDuckGo is the default web crawler over Hooray, Google, or Bing, to pick the private satisfying web searcher as the default. Snap Settings at that point open Safari and snap Web list. Passwords can be put away due to iCloud, Safari over the entire of contraptions in Settings. iPhone propose recommended question things, it is on as default yet if need not waste time with it. To stop goals following, you have to go to Settings to approach Safari and make changes there. For handling Safari and iCloud, if any glitch experienced refreshes the phone, otherwise go to the settings and adjust them subsequently concerning the error you are facing.

Safari shows pictures of most visited regions each time open another page. Apple presented Records application in 2017 for iOS 11. Safari preloads the guideline hit of the inquiry respect decides to pick stacking. Apple has added the capacity to utilize the camera to divert MasterCard to fill in a charge card. The capacity to get to iCloud Drive records can likewise be turned on or off in Safari.

Back to Mail open home. Go to the page you originated from.

The component is accessible on Macintosh's iOS 11 working framework, iPhone, iPad, and iPod Contact. Apple discharged iOS 11 on September 12, 2017, and the update will be accessible on September 13, 2017. The update is accessible in the U.S., Canada, Australia, New Zealand, the U.K., the Netherlands, Norway, Germany, Denmark, Norway, and the Netherlands. It will likewise be accessible in different nations not long from now. Apple has not reported designs to present the component in the U.K.

5.2 Home Screen and Display

There are a variety of options available on the home screen, such as turning on the night mode, making your screen dull, or zoom options to adjust the screen font size and rotation modes to present the screen in landscape or portrait modes. Whereas Sound can be adjusted using the side button, quick search and navigation can also be turned on.

Get the Dim View cloud scenic views a notable part of iOS 13's update is the latest feature-decreasing judgment. With two or three re-installed settings, the image can be darkened and changed whenever the dull mode is prompted.

Go to Backdrop Configurations at that stage and prosecute the "decreased appearance decreases landscape" flip is changed on. By then, press "Select New Settings" and select one from "photographs" or "Screen," which has a tiny cover picture in the lower right corner. By and by, whatever points the mode decrease is deeply involved; the perspective will go dreary in the same way. Improve the images on the home screen now because there is no more weight-sensitive emergence, a bit of a long press and force-contact exercise has changed. There are two different approaches to the revision of device photos. Just long-press the button and select "delete apps" in the spring folder, or long-press and move the emblem until even the spring-up list appears.

Easily introduce multiple features to the device. This concept has been used for a quiet time, so rather than only individually, little by little dragging each pledge into a planner will rapidly put them along. Long-press the application and drag it to the top of another image; by then, quickly tap several different implementations to form a combing social opportunity for use.

Enable dull mode go to configurations, click demonstrate and Splendor, and now turn on the Dim switch. It can change in almost the same manner, based on the period of the day or break/sunset usually.

Set the screen splendor, raise the Control Center by swiping down from the top left side of the screen, alter the Introduction Wonder slider, or go to configuration Open Showcase and Brilliance.

Standard or Zoomed Show Since iPhone 6 or more, 'have had the choice to choose between two objective alternatives. You can change the settings for a feature from standard or able to zoom. Switch between the two-in cases 'Adjusted Game Plan View'-go to Open Presentation and Splendor Settings and click Show Zoom and select Norm or Zoomed

Empower Genuine Tone Show to get the iPhone screen to normally modify its concealing equality and temperature to organize the surrounding light in the room, head to the Control Center, and long-press the Splendor Screen slider. Tap the Real Tone icon lead. You may also go to Settings to unlock Spotlight and Creativity and change the "Veritable Sound."

Sincere Sound, there's an alternative for Night Move to remove blue light, allowing the eyes to loosen up. Upload the Control Center by clicking the Grandstand magnificence slider and pick the Night Shift icon.

To adjust the standard text size, go to Settings Access View and Splendor; then, while changing the scale, pick the "Font Height" option to alter the width. Below 'Text Size,' he will also find a turn for incredible substance; switch it on in the incident that the system substance is too difficult to even recognize at night when browsing.

Quickly navigate to Wi-Fi settings by holding the Settings image to expose shortcut buttons to the power supply, powerful and flexible Information, Wi-Fi, and Bluetooth settings. Moving makes it incredibly fast to skip to the faraway locations.

Expel Stock Applications after the iOS 11 upgrade in 2017, and the company has been able to clear Apple's default features like Stocks, Compass, among many others. To do this, press and hold and keep the submission picture close for quite a while before it begins wriggling and then hit the "x" button a moment later to validate the judgment. To bring them back, a basic task for the developer is referred to in the Software Store.

Consider another setting like for all recent smart phones; iPhone has revamped the latest edition range. Current configurations to be created in Preferences then background. Here will notice a revived guarantee in both Static and Live contexts.

Yield and Spot Screen Catches for this take a display run; by then, a little Screen Catch Screen appears in the bottom left corner. Tap it and then use the conceivable outcomes that seemed to catch, create, or crop the image.

5.3 Messages, Emoji and Keyboard Tips

For iMessage and keyboard, several functions are available such as turning Memoji and Emoji on adjusting their shape and inventing your very new own stickers. Beside this, you can also get template stickers by the browser and clicking the globe icon on the keyboard via globe button you can select to work with built-in keyboards or gboards.

Memoji stickers: the choice is now to submit Memoji as fixed emoticon badges. Enable them by pressing the emoticon symbol on the console to test the answers openly. To screen a dynamically big proportion, press the three-bit icon, you may also scan the available animoji and Memoji as they appear here. Who is Memoji? Which is Memoji? The perfect technique for making an Animoji

In FaceTime call, using Memoji / Animoji: launch a FaceTime call and then click the little star icon in the base corner. Until taping long, the Memoji must be used.

Create Memoji: Apple developed a cute feature named Animoji for iPhone X. There's Memoji concisely. This lets you reveal your personalized Animoji creation. Open Notifications and launch an additional post. Tap the little monkey image and press "+" to render the character along these lines. This will also be necessary to alter the face form, skin tone, hair cover, eyebrows, jewelry, and many more at a very basic stage.

Memoji selfies: in these cases, when choosing the face of Memoji better than the entire picture, you should submit Memoji pictures with the abrogation face in Messages. Begin the message and click the camera image then click the start button for a limited period afterward. Choose Animoji concisely by clicking the monkey's head again. Choose Memoji and press 'x' and maintain the future-oriented camera structure.

Phase by phase guidelines for silent unambiguous conversations: In the first Texts Mailbox, you should dissimulate the alerts you should start taping "disseminate the bell." It is helpful whether the notification about a social occurrence is astonishingly straightforward and friendly.

Drawing and giving someone an image: in texts, persons created sketches can be sent as Apple Watch customers.

Tap the picture of the tiny app stores apart from the message involve participation. 'You can look at a little cardiac mark with two fingers on it over the screen, press it and start drawing some time later. To dynamically render the boring canvas simple, move the tiny lower bar across the drawing area upward till the frame is full.

Submit a picture to someone: apart from a Communications area of material knowledge, they'll see a tiny camera image. Tap it, and the full-screen camera code will be sent instantly. Tap the photo in the top left corner to get to the images from the presentation.

The easiest way to kiss anyone: in Texts, one should submit either a sketch or a picture, but create forms or templates to explore a kiss for the phone. To bring a smile, go to the plain linen with both fingers, where the heart is important to light up. To sever the hand, swipe down without raising the fingertips from the computer while pressing hard.

The strongest way to iMessages impacts: iOS 10 also introduced the opportunity to combine full-screen and air pocket effects for iMessage. After three years, more implications for iOS 13 are now starting.

To cope with these impacts, click and keep the picture after a message has been formed. Here, the results of adding them to the text may be adjusted between the insulating layer and device.

The best system to pick a message image: may choose the Markup or alter images easily before they are sent to iOS. To do this, pick an image and attach it to the post. Click on the picture before publishing, and you'll make or alter the choice to Markup.

The most popular strategy is to draw on a picture and give somebody a photo, then instead of drawing on a painting, click the camcorder button. Then the solution will be to log and draw a response, respectively.

The best way to address a request: double-tap on a specific post, and 'can you reveal a range of images involving a face, love, frustration, ha, and? When you pinch one, you add it to the other person's post on iOS to display. Again, crushing it will clear the reaction.

Step by step to iMessage applications: in every communication conversation, you can see the whole apps in iMessage in a toolbar at the bottom of the page. Swap left or right to locate the program you are looking for. If you do, you can see them in a slider above the solace eye.

Phase by phase District Exchanging Titles: You can easily exchange district inside a message by beginning some conversation or address list. Tap the tiny shock at the top near the name of the contact; click "I," and pick "share my region" or "submit my flow region" at that level.

What time: Display when a text has been sent by removing the button from the left side of the chat screen.

Speedy Voice message: If you click on the small micro button, you can start recording a human voice. Speedy Voice message Raise the hand to pause the rewind button and reveal it.

Sending push notifications step-by-step rules: iOS offers autonomous decision to organize Sending push notifications, considering a specific topic. In an identical menu, flip on the "Submit Read Transcripts" function.

See associations: Go to a message string at this point, tap the small triangle at the top to contact name, and tap "I." At the bottom of the display and any affiliations / photographs that have made the connection are seen at the bottom of the screen.

Press Settings Access Messages and glance down at "Mail Background" a little back. Here you can opt to keep the Messages indefinitely, a year or 30 days.

Inevitably, destroy Sound and video texts: Mac schedules them such that if a sound alert has been received, after two minutes, Mac eradicates them from the iPhone or iPad. If the message wants to be held, go to the Open Communications settings to display Sound Communications or text messages bits to adjust the "Start" function.

Deleted texts: Like in the previous, hoarding from the left-hand decision in the Texts category and press the "annihilate" alternative for a brief period afterward.

Increase the standard of display of sound messages: according to the traditional process, though, it may brawl the ability to turn and reply by raising a telephone to sound messages. To shut it off, enter and open notes in Preferences, and adjust Raise to Load.

Go one-gave: Snappy Kind's support iOS 13 makes one-move, stumbling on greater gadgets such as iPhoneXS Max. Click and hold the thumbnail of the globe to select the left or the correct screen. It receives the screen and transfers it next to the display. Return to full assessment by clicking the little jerk.

Submit iMessage as SMS: when the trouble is sending iMessages, you can decide to return iOS 13 and submit it as SMS. Go to Open Messages Settings and adjust the "Return as SMS" option.

Blue and white: Blue airbags are available for iMessages, and white for regular SMS communications.

Swipe to text the opportunity to text aid by swiping over the characters is one of the highlights of iOS 13. Start with the basic word of the term and type the others easily. Only keep the letter in a limited period anytime you require a double letter in the term before continuing with the swiping.

Using warmth as a touchpad: 3D Touch is gone, and the touchpad fuse can no longer be used by rubbing hard the screen. Or even again, you theoretically ought to press the space bar long to give a simple convergence point to pass the cursor around until you click along with the keyboard for a long time.

Show the device and stick to the standards of the program. Sooner or later, you can ask to select Settings to Enable General Consoles and fuse pariah comfort.

Simple text replacement, as with the previous year, iOS' main device projects produce short codes that are turned into complete words or descriptions. Go to Open General Snap Help Settings and come upon Text Replacement. We think it is interesting that we're a for an area that takes up at every stage where we erroneously spell "username" even an extra "s" at the top.

Emoji's choosing cover with every time spending just a few years, Emoji has the option of adjusting the skin color. To get to them, go to emoticon help by tapping the image; at this point, you have to use the long push on the emoticon. They can demonstrate that it has flexible covering equivalents.

Going to other consoles Emoji after various platforms have theoretically been added, click the photo on the screen for a long time. You can get a sprung up list of options you should use. Taping the image of the globe will turn easily with assistance.

Strangle comfort tends to work over the console of Apple requires an accumulation of character energy to be checked before taping the buttons. Might avoid it

Debilitate boost capitalization; all solace letters were advanced before iOS 9, whether it hit a moving key or not. The console should display the letters in a lower state before long, while the change is off. You do not need to bother with this; you can complicate it by pressing Ease and turning off the "Lower Case Keys" button to unlock Control settings.

5.4 Camera and Photos

With the advancement of technology, camera, and photo technology have also been updated by Apple by providing a better user interface and introducing features for live photography video recording and retina camera features.

One new interface in the camera application is the ability to rapidly shoot a video inside the Photograph mode. To make an alleged Slofie, change to the Moderate Mo elective and essentially tap the camera switcher image to change to Front Camera. One of the new iPhone's camera movements is Shrewd HDR, which helps bolster tints, light, and detail in troublesome lighting conditions. Apple's new iPhone11 Star Max is available now in the U.S. and Canada for $999. It's the first iPhone with a screen resolution of 5.7 inches (Retina display) and has a screen refresh rate of 1.5 megapixels (Retina). It has a rear-facing camera with a 12-megapixel camera with an 8-megapixel sensor.

With the new iPhones, you can change the lightning sway's nature in the wake of shooting the Picture shot. Live Photographs are dynamic. When picking one of the Live Photograph impacts, it saves it on the phone as a video, not an image.

You can shoot 1080p moderate development at 240fps and tap "Record Moderate motion" to record the most extraordinary speed decision. The iPhone 5S comes with a larger screen with a screen resolution of 8 megapixels and a screen refresh rate of 0.7 seconds. It also has a faster 4GB version with 2GB of memory. The new iPhone 5C has a screen size of 8.7 inches. It is the biggest improvement over the iPhone 4S and comes with an 8" screen with a screen-sized screen-mounted touch screen. It has a 7" screen and a 6" screen.

Go to Photographs application, open a Live Photograph, and swipe it up to reveal three new impacts. Long press the camera application image, and choose to take a Picture Selfie, Take Representation, or Record Video, or Take Video. The best strategy to quickly dispatch various camera modes is to long-press the photo and tap on the "play" image on the essential picture and a short time later Tap on the offer image. Step-by-step guidelines to apply a live photograph to a photo are given below. The final step is to search for and select a specific image to share with a specific person or group of people to make a video.

The video can then be shared in the form of a split-screen of a single image, or as a montage of three separate video clips, as well as a single video of two separate images of the same person, or a combination of the two images taken at the same time, to share as part of a larger montage or video montage. The full video will be available later this week on Apple's mobile software.

Siri adds the ability to fix photos, transfer blasts, and see where photos were taken. Apple's new iPhone 5S has several new features. Photos can now be transferred, broken up, cropped, and resized. Users can also use the camera's Time-Pass mode to shoot a period pass video with almost no effort. Siri can now solicit photos from users to bring them to her for her to look at, and she can search for them. It can also take a gander at photos subject to their information and models to see where they were taken and what they were snapped in, among other features. The new Photos app is available on the iPhone 5, 5S, 6, 6S, plus the iPad, iPad mini and the iPad mini with Retina display. It costs $39.99 for the full-size iPhone 5 and 6 plus $39 for the 32GB version with 32GB storage. It is available now in the U.S. and Canada.

iPhone 5 has several features that let users change presentations on the fly. To switch between cameras, tap the little "1x" image to switch between wide, ultra-wide, and zoom. With night mode enabled, iPhone consequently sets the presentation time. When tapping the "Years" decision, the photographs application can quickly scour during that time by swiping left and directly the thumbnail. Back to Mail online home. Back to the page you came from. Back to the page, you came from the page your phone came from, and the best way to use it.

5.5 Control Centre and Lock Screen Tips

In the notification center, there is an option to allow or disallow the notification from different apps and built-in software of the device. It is on the user to interpret and restrict the notifications from the apps, which he does not want to see. There are some additional settings for calendar and alarm notifications on the display menu along with their icon adjustments.

Reconfigure commands to change the order for these controls, click the button the three-bar icon of whatever force you choose to push, push it wherever, anywhere, until you have it, to anywhere you want it.

Have additional settings: like the former version of iOS, Control Center functions may be added and disabled. To access Control Position Settings, press Modify Settings then select the controls you want to use.

Turn on tightly and personally: the usability device has, of course, only four choices. On the possibility that the long press would extend it, a full-screen command with two more choices will be offered. Tap the hotspot picture to activate it.

Change the light/spot quality: can be turned on by accessing the Control Group and taping the flash file, utilizing it as illumination. To switch the Splendor, click the badge for a long period to alter the full-screen toggle.

Turn easily to the Sound. Another new aspect is to adjust the playing place of music. Apple Music or Spotify performs music, or anywhere you move the music power over for a long time or just tap through the little illustration in the top corner. This creates a spring that reveals accessible devices that can play. It may be connected to earpieces, N.F.C., Apple T.V.T.V., iPhone, or any airplay unit.

Real screen recording is one of the choices introduced in 2018 that can be applied to Monitor Location.

Ensure the screen stretches, open the screen position, and click the picture inside a thin white ring after a sincere white flow. It will document all that happens on-screen beginning now and within a fair period. When installed, click the control again, and it will then transfer a video to the Photographs program.

Note fresh center admonitions appear as usual on the lock screen, as default. You will easily find the more trained ones you have checked or discarded, swipe up the central focus of the lock screen, and display "See Middle". Be cautious not to launch the count prematurely, 'mainly open your device and go to your home screen

Simple warnings click the tiny "x" throughout the corner of the screen with Alert Center and touch the "responsive."

Set a colorful clock instead of scraping to the time application; may press the clock icon forward, move up or down on the full screen to test anywhere in the middle of a second or two hours.

Home Package gadgets instructions Open the control position and press on the tiny picture that seems like a building shortly after.

Power switch, there is a lock screen click as a webcam for display on / off. Click it, and get a flash.

Wake tap of example, iPhone 11 can be shifted by clicking on the device if necessary later. It will light up, and the lock screen will be shown.

Unlock camera via lock screen Instead of this tap. Apple has melted a video icon at the top right of the lock screen on the baseline. Click it, and the app heads straight to the phone.

Lift phone to open: bring the phone up to open up and send each of the Lock screen warnings. To assassinate this part or go to Display and splendor environments, shift Lift to rise.

The perfect approach for today is to show lock screen contraptions. Swipe the lock button from left to right.

Brisk Response When an alert falls in-based on how the client participates-you should respond easily before opening the particular application. To do so, pull down the notification to show the gestures. On the other side, from either the home screen, you can click the alert and tap "response."

Opening directions on the home screen using Face ID consumers can unlock their iPhone, in any situation, without undertaking on the main screen. To do that, grab the handset, and the hook icon on the top of the device displays it explicitly. The program's default display should not be taken away from the off possibility of the tap in any event.

IOS 10 is the perfect strategy for incorporating and includes a Currently View page that can show devices from any program that supports. It has usually stayed unchanged from now on and into the near future. To install, delete or upgrade, test the Today discovery (swipe to the lock screen or first home screen), and then explore the foundation's rights a short time later. Tap the button to adjust the contraptions and the query

Accumulated lock screen admonitions can delete a specific example or warning obtained by swiping more from the alternative to the left or pressing "clear" or "simple all" afterward.

5.6 Notifications and Restrictions

Control centers have a variety of features introduced for special and disabled people, which can be adjusted by approaching the settings button. In contrast, the control panel can also serve multiple functions, including screen recording, adjusting the brightness, setting up facial id personal security, and improved performance management.

Apple's latest iOS 13 includes multiple lock screen update sets. The operating system arranges programs into separate groups, both useful and ineffectively organized.

Battery and wireless charging features are briefly described and methods to attach them with a power supply with the alternative tips mentioned to charge fast. Users may opt to pay for specific programs and calls. The operating system iOS 13 introduces a separate update kit to iOS 11, iOS 13. It allows users to submit advisories from specific apps to Notification Centers without alerting them to vibration or device or illuminating a lock screen with vibration or even lighting the computer. The new program also provides the option to "delete" the device as users try information that does not suit the customer's needs. The screen configuration interface provides a new "Calendar" feature to restrict the viewing duration of some programs, and other duration ranges for other items. It will also restrict the amount of information a device will view on the computer, for instance, when a consumer sees an image or a video and restrict the duration of a notification to a couple of seconds.

5.7 Battery and Wireless Charging Explained

IOS specifically shows which applications use the squeeze most. Low Power Mode (Settings > Battery) helps to lower power consumption. Buy a remote charger to use the remote charging features of the iPhone. Any Qi charger will work, but for Apple's 7.5W charging, you will need one upgraded. Under the better battery, the most recent 24 hours are displayed, with separate tabs at around 14 days. There are two tabs that display the average use of batteries. One displays the battery level, and screen-on and screen-off behavior display differently. Under the screen-On and Screen-Off diagrams, the average battery life is displayed. The battery level is the average battery life over the past 24 hours; different tabs display average battery use over the last 14 days, based on normal use.

5.8 Notes, Maps, and Apple Music Tips

Notes, maps, and apple music are user-friendly apps in your phone that can be adjusted according to your mood, and requirements can be back linked with online portals of iCloud.

You can set plans to add notes or mark locations on maps easily.

Before this, there is an option to add music to the iTunes from online stores or add it by earning a download from a safari or attaching it with your pc.

Mail tips

There's a hung Mail remember for iOS Mail that licenses to react to messages inside the string rather than simply the latest one. Swiping from the alternative to leave reveals quick exercises to let do different things. The best strategy for new messages in Mail is to go to any of the inboxes via the Post office application and tap the little drift image with three bars lessening in size. Swipe left on any email in the inbox and continue swiping to make it the whole way over the screen. In an open email that is being made, pull down from the title to dock the email can keep doing this and swipe aside to close the email. The option to have various messages in a rush at once is advantageous if you are exceptionally associated with explaining to someone and, by then, need to send a speedy email in the center. Swiping from alternative to left, tap "More" and select "Prompt me" from the overview to print the email. In inbox swipe from left to alternative to reveal a "Read" image.

Using Mail Drop on iOS 11 was familiar with Macintosh operating system X with letting successfully send immense email associations utilizing iCloud. Search: Drag down in inbox to reveal a chase box. Users can now have the option to look entire inbox for a catchphrase rather than just To, From, Subject. Indoor aides: For the main go through in Apple Guides, iOS 11 enabled indoor wanting to find a way around fundamental malls. It is continuously evolved starting now and into the foreseeable future and can endeavor it in a whole host of standard overall air terminals. The iOS Mail application can associate an impressive record (5GB to 20GB) associated with up to 5GB of data. The app is free to download from the App Store and is available on Apple's iOS 11 software. The App Store is free for download from Apple's App Store.

Apple has included new 3D structures inside its Road View elective in Guides in iOS 13. Head to San Francisco in the Guides application and tap the new optic image to see a Road View-like view.

The mission for an extensive city like London or New York taps the "Flyover" elective. By then, ought to just move the device and look at the city in a 3D virtual 3D view. It's confined to explicit urban zones and territories in the guide's app for the time being, however.

The company developed its own Guides application, complete with Flyover 3D types of noteworthy urban regions.

Notes:

Long push on the Notes application image and pick "New Agenda" and a short time later start making rundown immediately. In Safari, tap the Offer catch to save joins, for instance, an association or report to another or existing Note. There's furthermore a Connections program in Notes that sorts out associations in a solitary view. On an iOS contraption that is not invigorated to 9.3 or later, it won't choose to get to it on that device. The best strategy, to share and collaborate on observes, is to share notes and collaborate with others. Back to the home screen, and then go back to the page you came from. The best way to use the Notes app is to open the app and long push it and then long push the note image.

Apple Music:

Go to Settings click Music and a short time later switch off "Show Apple Music" Directly when going to the application; it will simply watch music rather than the music available on the organization.

To see all the tunes, assortments, and playlists that included from the Apple Music list, basically tap the Library tab from the application's menu bar along the base. The best strategy to find Apple's curated playlists: The "For" tab found in the menu bar is the place that can go to find music suggestions hand-picked by the Apple music gathering. The Top Graphs portion in the Peruse tab gives every one of the types of playlist. Go back online to the server and then Back To the page you came from. To see the music you bought from iTunes, including Cds that tore, simply tap the Downloaded Music tab.

Apart from Beats 1, Apple Music offers radio stations that rely upon sorts and different subjects. Apple Music can arrange assortments to add to playlists or share through social networks. It's also possible to download an assortment to a library for separated tuning in. The best strategy to find the Beats 1 radio station is to tap the Radio tab in the menu bar along the base, and a while later tap the Beats1 thumbnail. Back to Mail online home.

Back to the page you came from. Â Back To the page you came from. The full guide can be found at the bottom of the page. Back to the site, you came to. Back to the page, you can share an assortment through Twitter, Facebook, or other social networks, such as Instagram and Twitter. It can be downloaded to a playlist or added to an old or new playlist or added to a Play Next line. The best technique to make a station from a tune is to make it reliant on that specific tune.

Tap on any tune, and after that from the music controls menu (tap it along the base to make it adventure into a full-screen card), select the catch with the three spots in the lower corner. Like tunes and assortments, can confer an artisan to a buddy utilizing relational associations and advising applications. Apple Music can arrange tunes have to check out while in a rush. The best technique to download a tune to the library for disengaged tuning is to tap the little" image" by then hitting the cloud download image. The song can also be shared via Facebook, Twitter, or other social media sites, such as Instagram and Twitter. Back to Mail online home. The best way to add a song to a playlist is to go to the Playlist and select which playlist (old or new) you'd like to add to. The most popular way to share a song is to share it with a friend via Twitter, Facebook, or Instagram.

5.9 Buttons, Gesture, and Control

The power button slide button and volume button are something more than the names they serve for multiple purposes along which the important once are gesture control and enabling Siri with voice recognition to work on your command. Hold the volume up button and the power button together, and it will bolt a screen of anything which is in plain view. Switch between applications, speedy if you have to switch between applications quickly, just take from left to legitimately on the base of the screen where the bar consistently appears. Press and hold the wake/lay catch on the correct side of the phone until the Siri interface jumps up on the screen. No continuous home catch suggests no progressively two-fold tapping the home catch to see s starting at now used applications. By and by slide to control off Apple Pay: What is Apple Pay? How does it work, and how can you set it up? What is the best way to get your hands on an iPhone X.S.X.S. or X? See here for all the latest news on how to get Apple Pay on your iPhone and iPad. The best phone screen protector: The iPhone 5S, XS, and XS Max can protect against scratches and dings. The iPhone 6, XR, X, and X.R.X.R. can protect from scratches and sun damage.

5.10 Payment Tips for Apple

Any access or purchase done with apple products or iPhone can be done apple payment methods via Apple wallet. Directions to use Apple Pay Installments to certify portions on a near to Macintosh can use Apple Pay on iPhone. Turn on "Grant Installments on Macintosh" to ensure this is on; go to Settings click Wallet, and Apple Payment application. Directions to change the default Apple Pay card to select the Default Card need go to Settings open Wallet and Apple Pay. If you simply have one card, it will be easy to handle the default card.

Conclusion

As everyone notes, the iPhone is the most widely purchased device and product brand in the world with the largest proportion of happy users. Apple provides user-friendly apps and tools that can be quickly created and used to make the world a global city just a click away.

Tap the bid icon at the base of the software on the page you are referring to. Tap the correct catch to share with you via Mail, Twitter or Airdrop, etc. For example, if you tap Mail, a different mail message will be shown on the subject line pre-populated with the name of the site you visit and the body. Just type your message text, flexibly enter your mate's email, and then press the Send button.

Various manufacturers are importing Apple products and parts worldwide. The AAPL re-appropriated the conference for monetary purposes. Steve Jobs initially hired the current CEO, Tim Cook, to improve the integrity of the organization. Cook through the number of vendors in the area in order to avoid duplication. The development of IOS has made Apple a very serious and successful company. According to the Bloomberg survey, the company spent $10.5 billion on a graceful chain from the introduction of robots to sorting machines. The investigation said that Apple's popularity had made it a profitable and prosperous company. Electronic mail back home, please. Apple Competition in the market will eventually add new phones to the iPhone users' wish list by adding the iPhone 12 series. It is believed that iPhone fans have a huge selection of iPhone episodes, originally released on January 20, 2012. Get off on the list. Get off on the list. Go back to the Internet.

Weight and thickness are the most noticeable improvements. IPhone11 Pro handles over 11 grams of XS. This more powerful beltline is responsible for the proposed four-hour battery gain. The IP68 water resistance was planned to be four meters instead of two meters for 30 minutes. The 5.8-inch iPhone11 Screen Size Strategy is immaculately lucrative in the palm of my hand, and I do not have to stretch my fingers to any part of the frame. There are, however, energizing preventive steps, most of which irritate the inability to access the USB-C terminal. The screen is 5.7 inches long, and the screen has a resolution of 5.6 inches. It is got a 5.2-inch screen thick. In one go, it can hold a full load.

All Apple stores, Apple.com and licensed Apple affiliates have access to and access to Apple's own cases. AppleCare+ extends your iPhone or iPad coverage from 90 days (including any device you purchase) to two years and offers unlimited mobile and individually qualified support. Many instances have an external screen, while others represent both the cell phone or tablet and the computer itself. The business offers a wide range of third-party iPhone and iPad distribution and case distributors.